ATHENS CITY SCHOOLS

D1404025

Wild Animals,
Gentle Women

Illustrated with line drawings
by Paul Facklam
and with photographs

By the same author
Frozen Snakes and Dinosaur Bones:
Exploring a Natural History Museum

Wild Animals, Gentle Women

Margery Facklam

Harcourt Brace Jovanovich, New York and London

The author and publisher wish to thank the following for permission
to reprint the copyrighted material listed below:

Education Development Center, Newton, Massachusetts, for nine lines
from "Magic Words" from *Songs and Stories of the Netsilik Eskimo.*
Text copyright © 1967, 1968 Education Development Center, Inc.

Harper & Row, Publishers, Inc., for the quotations in Chapter Seven
which are from *Lads Before the Wind* by Karen Pryor.
Copyright © 1975 by Karen Pryor.

J. B. Lippincott Company for the quotations in Chapter Three
which are from *The Lady and the Panda* by Ruth Harkness.
Copyright 1938 by Carrick & Evans, Inc. Copyright © renewed 1966 by
Mrs. Nelson Anderson, Mrs. Warren R. Burdick, and Mr. James W. McCombs.

Library of Congress Cataloging in Publication Data

Facklam, Margery.
Wild animals, gentle women.

Bibliography: p.
Includes index.
SUMMARY: Describes the experiences of eleven women
who study animal behavior: Belle Benchley, Ruth Harkness,
Jane Goodall, [etc.]
1. Women ethologists—Biography—Juvenile literature.
[1. Ethologists.   2. Animals—Habits and behavior.
3. Zoologists.]   I. Facklam, Paul.   II. Title.
QL26.F3   591.5 [B] [920]   77-88961
ISBN 0-15-296987-X

For Mim, my sister,
who became my best friend
in spite of snakes in the bedroom,
and for Dave, my brother,
the real animal lover in the family,
who helped feed the porcupines

and in memory of our parents,
who never discouraged any
of our interests, no matter
what directions they took

Contents

Chapter One
Talking to the Animals
11

Chapter Two
Belle Benchley: Zoo Director
16

Chapter Three
Ruth Harkness and the *Bei-Shung*
27

Chapter Four
Jane Goodall and the Community of Chimpanzees
39

Chapter Five
Kay McKeever and a Parliament of Owls
51

Chapter Six
Hope Buyukmihci and the Keepers of the Stream
61

Chapter Seven
Karen Pryor and the Creative Porpoise
72

Chapter Eight
Eugenie Clark and the Sleeping Sharks
82

Chapter Nine
Dian Fossey and the Gentle Giants
93

Chapter Ten
Biruté Galdikas and the Red Apes
103

Chapter Eleven
Leone Pippard, Heather Malcolm, and the Sea Canaries
113

Chapter Twelve
Is Animal Watching for You?
124

Bibliography
129

Organizations to Help You Learn about Animal Watching
133

Index
135

Wild Animals,
Gentle Women

Chapter One
Talking to
the Animals

In the very earliest time,
when both people and animals lived on earth,
a person could become an animal if he wanted to
and an animal could become a human being.
Sometimes they were people
and sometimes animals
and there was no difference.
All spoke the same language.
That was the time when words were like magic.

From *Songs and Stories of the Netsilik Eskimo*

But the magic time is gone, and we can't talk to the animals. We can only guess how they feel, how their senses compare to ours, or how intelligent they are.

We say that owls are wise. Beavers are industrious. Dolphins are smart. Gorillas are fierce, foxes are sly. Snakes are evil, lions are proud.

But are they? How can we really know what an animal is like? Everyone has opinions about animals. Some people think animals react like machines, thinking nothing, feeling nothing. Others go to the opposite extreme and believe that animals are just like people, maybe even smarter.

Ever since we human animals appeared on earth, we have used other animals—their flesh for food, their skins for clothing and shelter, and their bones for weapons and tools. We taught them to help us farm, to provide us with transportation, to carry our messages, to entertain us and give us pleasure as our pets. And we watched them, loving some of them, fearing others.

When we see an animal do something, we explain it the only way we know—in human terms. Our own feelings and reactions get in the way. For example, if we put out bread for birds to eat and a squirrel takes the bread, we call the squirrel a thief. We say he is sneaky. When we see a hawk swooping down on a smaller bird, we call the hawk a murderer.

That kind of thinking is called anthropomorphic, which simply means assuming that an animal has the same thoughts and feelings as we humans.

When zoology was new, it was a science of collecting and organizing animals into systematic groups. Museums began to spring up just to hold all the animals that scientists collected, named, measured, and described. This was useful and necessary, but no matter how many dead animals are collected, they can't tell us much about the way animals spend their lives.

In the 1800s, many of the zoologists and naturalists who were out collecting with guns and traps also become interested in the animals' behavior. But much of what they reported was anthropomorphic. They fell into the habit of describing what animals did in human terms.

As late as 1922, a well-known naturalist, William Hornaday, wrote a book called *The Mind and Manners of Wild Animals.* In it he said that wolves were crafty, dangerous, and cruel. He told big-game hunters they would find lions courageous, confident, and very reliable, but that tigers were nervous, suspicious, treacherous, and uncertain.

Now we realize that that kind of labeling makes about as much sense as saying that all plumbers are confident and reliable, or that all politicians are nervous, suspicious, and treacherous.

But as zoologists wondered more and more why animals did certain things and how they learned, American scientists in particular began to study animals in laboratories full of the newest equipment. They even earned the nickname "rat runners" because they ran rats through mazes to see how fast the animals learned.

They found out how animals breathe, how their muscles work, how they digest their food, and which parts of their brains produce pleasure or pain. They even counted and diagramed the patterns of feathers on birds and the fur on mammals. They really learned about animals from the inside out. But we were still saying things like, "Wolves are vicious."

Fortunately, human animals are a curious lot, and scientists in particular are like the python in Kipling's *Jungle Book*—full of insatiable curiosity. They never stop asking why or how. Why do birds sing? Why do beavers build dams? Why do gorillas beat their chests? Why are dolphins always friendly to man? How does one bee tell another where the pollen is? How does a duckling keep track of its mother in a barnyard full of ducks? How does a baby seal find its mother on a beach covered with seals?

Questions like those were the beginning of a new science called *ethology,* the study of animal behavior. It is very much like the old-fashioned nature study, dealing as it does with animals in the wild. But it goes further. It asks different questions. It uses scientific methods to piece together a picture of an animal's life: how it courts, mates, and raises its young; how it defends its territory; how it handles aggression—in other words, how an animal gets along in its own society.

Konrad Lorenz has been called the father of ethology. His work has shown that behavior patterns are inherited, just like red hair or blue feathers or curved tusks. A wolf cub taken from its mother and raised by humans will still greet other wolves in the age-old tradition of all wolves. It did not learn that greeting from the humans, but knew it anyway. If a beaver is raised in captivity and has never seen a beaver lodge, it can still build a lodge like any other beaver's.

Do we humans also have behavior patterns that are inherited from generation to generation? According to many ethologists, the way we bow or nod our heads when we greet each other, or the way we back down when a bully threatens us, or the way our hair bristles on the back of the neck when we are frightened are all patterns of behavior that had their beginnings millions of years ago.

Sally Carrighar, a writer and naturalist, said, "In the natural behavior of other animals we discover much about ourselves: our social life and play, our passions and aggressions, our patterns of courtship, parenthood and sex."

She went on to explain that animals, of course, do not always do the right and perfect thing, even for their own survival. Just because we study animals does not mean we should imitate them.

But she added, "The last few recent years are the only time in all history when human beings have had a chance to compare our own behavior with accurately described behavior of the animals from whom we had descended . . . or ascended."

The science of ethology clearly shows us that man is united with all animals. And from these studies we get useful ideas about the unlearned behavior of babies and the ways in which we humans learn.

Thousands of people spend their lives with animals, working with them or studying them. Many of these people are women. This book is about eleven women who became animal watchers. Some are famous, others are little known. Some are trained scientists who knew from the time they were young that they would work with animals. Others never intended to become involved with animals at all, but found their lives totally changed because of an encounter with an animal. Some traveled to distant foreign countries, and others never left home. Some learned from animals in zoos, some in their own backyards, and others in oceans and jungles.

All of these women share several traits. They are patient, strong, and capable. And each of them found one thing to be true: The more they watch and the more they think they know about an animal, the more questions they find to ask.

Chapter Two
Belle Benchley:
Zoo Director

Teddy, a baboon, swung along the wire fence outside of the monkey cages. His young mate scrambled after him on all fours, her long arms reaching out along the ground to keep up.

Four keepers banged trash-can lids together, waved brooms, and shouted as they worked to head the animals back to their own cages. Although the two baboons had escaped from their cages, they had not yet noticed that they could be completely free simply by leaping over the high fence surrounding the outdoor area. They were much too busy discovering the other caged baboons and monkeys and staying out of the keepers' reach.

Belle Benchley, the new zoo director, heard the wild commotion as she was getting out of her car that sunny morning. At first she thought that the keepers might only be chasing rats that often scurried around the cages looking for scraps of food. But when she opened the gate and went inside, she realized she was in the middle of a great escape.

It is hard to say who was the most startled—Belle, the keepers, or the runaway baboons.

"Stop! Go back. Baboons loose!" shouted the keepers. But Belle did not move.

Baboons are not cute. People think of them as the bad guys of the primates because they are aggressive with their large, ferocious-looking teeth. Most anyone would be tempted to leave them to whatever territory they chose to defend.

It was apparent that the keepers did not think the zoo's new director would be any help at all. Belle certainly did not look like a person who might be able to run a zoo, let alone catch a baboon. She looked more like a cookie-baking grandma in a Walt Disney movie. Her hair was pulled back into a bun, and her round, pleasant face looked all of its forty-five years. She was plump and not built for dashing after baboons.

What the keepers did not know was that Belle had been quietly making friends with Teddy. She said afterward, "He had been kind enough to put his big hand through the wire of his cage and accept fruit from me. He had also allowed me, when no one else was present, to clasp his hand; and he had gently taken mine in his, smacking his lips together, uttering low but friendly grunts, and showing me in many ways that he accepted me as a pretty good-type baboon."

When Teddy saw Belle standing there so calmly, with nothing in her hands that looked threatening, the young baboon started to gallop toward her. The men yelled their warnings again, but Belle did not move.

Later, Belle told the keepers that she had stood still not because she was afraid or even because she was brave, but only because there was nowhere to go. If she had gone back out the gate, the baboons would have scampered after her.

Teddy stopped a few steps in front of the zoo director. He smacked his lips and made grunting sounds as he held out his hand. As Belle took the little paw, the head keeper quickly stepped up and grasped the baboon's other paw, and together they led Teddy back to his cage. Teddy's mate scurried after them. The baboons almost looked like two children happy to be home again.

Belle was grateful for a friendship that had helped solve what could have been a dangerous situation.

Not long after the baboon escape, a man ran into Belle's office one day shouting, "Hurry, a rattlesnake is loose."

Remembering that day, Belle said that her first reaction was only to smile because visitors seem to think every snake is a rattlesnake. But she followed the excited man to the reptile house.

And a rattlesnake *was* loose. Stretched along the top of a cage, above Belle's head, was a large, poisonous snake. Something had to be done at once. She did not mind touching a snake, but like any sensible person, she didn't want to pick up a poisonous one.

"He lay perfectly still, hoping not to be discovered," said Belle. "I stretched forth my arm slowly. He noticed the movement and raised his head about an inch." At that moment she grabbed the snake tightly behind its head. Its heavy body swung off the cage and hung down until it touched the floor.

She carried the snake through the crowd and upstairs, wondering all the time how she would let go of it without being bitten. She managed to get a snake box from a shelf with her free hand and lower the snake into it.

"I released my hold so gradually he was free before he knew it. Then I banged the door shut."

Thinking about it later, Belle said, "I do not wish this to happen often, but I am glad that it did once, for it showed me that in an emergency, I could make myself do what had to be done."

After that, there was no doubt in the mind of any keeper that Belle would do what had to be done to manage a man-made jungle.

Belle Benchley never intended to become a zoo director. In 1925, when the San Diego Zoo was only a small, three-year-old park, Belle needed a job to support herself and her teen-age son. An employment agency sent her to the new zoo to apply for a job as book-keeper. She knew almost nothing about keeping financial accounts, and even less about zoos. But she got the job, she worked hard, and she learned quickly.

As bookkeeper, she was paying bills for such things as a gross of frogs, tons of watermelons and hay, truckloads of stale bread, and fifty-gallon drums of cod liver oil. On her lunch hours she began to walk around the zoo to see the animals that were eating this odd assortment of food. Each day she spent more and more time with the animals.

Then one day the bird keeper became ill, and Belle was asked to fill in for him and feed the birds. She worked with such enthusiasm that a year and a half later she was managing the entire zoo. Years later she explained: "I was a good housekeeper. I did what had to be done."

The San Diego Zoo is known as the "zoo man's zoo" because it is one of the best zoological parks in the world. The area has perfect zoo weather, so the animals can be outdoors all year. When Belle took it over, the small zoo in Balboa Park was home for about five hundred birds, mammals, and reptiles. The grounds were unde-veloped, and the zoo staff worried from day to day whether they would be able to afford to feed the animals.

But under Belle's careful direction, the zoo began to thrive and grow. The founders had decided at the beginning to exhibit the animals in family groups whenever possible. This led to a baby boom, and the San Diego Zoo became known for its baby animals. Belle found that she had animals to trade or sell to other zoos, and the San Diego collection began to include some strange animals.

Someone shipped a tiny tapir from South America. A tapir is related to the horses and rhinoceroses, but it looks more like a pig with a short, movable trunk. This strange baby was a scrawny, bony, weak little creature when it came to Belle. She described it as an animal "wearing a soft suit of sparse hair that seemed several sizes too large."

Caring for the tapir became a tiring, tedious job. The baby would not eat, so Belle began arriving at the zoo at seven in the morning to cook cereal for him. She stayed late every evening, coaxing him to try some food. She would have taken him home, but he was too large and clumsy to fit easily into her car.

Late one afternoon, when only a few visitors were left in the park, Belle was in the tapir's enclosure. She had named him Mickey, and she was urging the still raggedy-looking animal to eat. A sailor, leaning against a tree, had been watching for some time. Finally, he walked over to the fence and said, "Lady, if you want that tapir to live, you ought to dig her a real dirty mud hole where she can wallow and sleep."

Belle was astounded, but apparently this sailor had seen tapirs do just that in South America. She was so discouraged that she was ready to try anything to make the animal more content.

She called to the janitor and a bus driver, and the three of them grabbed picks and shovels and began hacking at the ground in the enclosure that was as hard as cement. When they had chopped a shallow hole, they filled it with water. Mickey headed right for the water. He rolled over, rubbed his back in the wet, sloppy mud, and wallowed with obvious pleasure.

Mickey was no problem after that. He ate and grew, and for all the years both he and Belle were at the zoo, Mickey ran to the fence to greet his friend whenever she whistled.

Belle cared about the animals. She made sure that each keeper on the staff wanted to be there more than anywhere else and cared about the animals as much as she.

She had to learn to be ready for any emergency, like the evening she was called out of a movie to retrieve a seal from a lady's bathtub. After weeks of heavy rain, the zoo had flooded, and the fence around the seal pool broke. Twenty-six happy seals swam down the gullies and into the streets of San Diego. The police answered dozens of phone calls from concerned citizens and passed the messages on to the zoo director. One of the seals had barked at a woman's front door and waddled into the living room when the door was opened. The surprised hostess finally herded the seal into the bathroom to wait in the tub until Belle identified him.

Belle Benchley, Director of the San Diego Zoo, shown here with two of the babies that have made her zoo famous. (San Diego Zoo photo)

One Christmas Eve, just as Belle was leaving for home, the keeper of the reptiles called her to look at a sick Galapagos tortoise. These animals are enormous, weighing up to several hundred pounds. When Belle saw the tortoise, she wasn't sure it was even alive. It looked cold and limp.

She and the keeper hoisted the animal into a wheelbarrow and took it to her office. They placed a pair of chairs together, making a bridge over a floor furnace, and hauled the tortoise onto them. The keeper went home, and Belle, not knowing what else to do, mixed some medicine. She put alcohol, mineral oil, and castor oil into a cup. She pried open the turtle's mouth with the handle of a toothbrush and poured the warm mixture into the animal's mouth.

"The turtle was either too dead to care, or he liked it," she said.

But he swallowed it, and Belle went home. The next morning she quite expected to see a dead tortoise. Instead, her office looked as though a muddy storm had blown through it. There was the tortoise—his nose running, his cold broken. He was still not looking the picture of health, but he was at least alive enough to turn over the wastebasket and chairs and tromp over everything.

Belle's office served as baby-care center and hospital many times before the zoo built their well-equipped animal hospital.

As the zoo grew, so did Belle's reputation as the "zoo lady." And the animals that brought her the most fame and joy were her gorillas.

In 1930, there were only three gorillas in captivity in the United States. One was in the Bronx Zoo in New York, one was in Washington, D.C., and the third was in Philadelphia. Very little was known about these animals, the largest of the primates.

A famous team of explorers, Martin and Osa Johnson, had captured two young gorillas in the rain forests of the Belgian Congo, and they were looking for a good home for the animals.

All the large zoos had put in offers for the gorillas, huge sums of money that the San Diego Zoo could not hope to match. But Belle was sure her zoo would be the best home of all. She wrote a long letter to Mr. Johnson, not trying to buy the animals but to sell him on the San Diego Zoo. She told him about the great, roomy outdoor cages, built with plenty of space for the animals to play and climb. She told him of the perfect zoo weather and the abundance of fresh food that was always available.

The Johnsons had checked dozens of zoos, but when they heard about the San Diego Zoo, they cabled Belle that the gorillas were hers.

It was an exciting day when the two gorillas arrived. Belle said, "I was overwhelmed with the responsibility that had fallen upon my shoulders, my responsibility to science, to the animals. So I began that night to write a gorilla diary. In it I set down the things I observed, whether or not I undertsood them, whether or not my conclusions were valuable."

It was the same method used many years later by Jane Goodall as she watched chimpanzees in their natural territory, and the same method other scientists now use as they watch animals in the wild. But Belle watched in the city, in the zoo.

She wrote about the thrilling day when the two gorillas arrived: "I had seen gorillas, but I was totally unprepared for the sight which met my eyes when Mbongo and Ngagi arrived and solemnly marched out, one behind the other, into the sunlight."

Mbongo was the younger and smaller of the two gorillas, and he often hesitated, waiting for the older Ngagi, before he tried anything new. Belle said she often saw the older gorilla touch the shoulder of his younger companion and with a warning grunt stop him before he stepped forward to examine something they had not seen before.

Everyone on the zoo staff agreed that the gorillas were to be allowed as much freedom from human interference as they could be given; they were to be treated like gorillas. Belle came to know the gorillas better than anyone else. Each morning before she went to her office, she stopped to watch the two big animals. She took a bunch of grapes with her the first morning, but when she called to the gorillas, they ignored her. She stood back, leaned against a tree, and began to eat the grapes herself, one by one.

Ngagi's mouth watered, but the older gorilla would not go near the director. Instead, he motioned to Mbongo, who grunted and walked to the fence. Belle stepped forward, holding a grape between her fingers.

"He put his big lips to the wire," she said, "and I hesitated before pushing my fingers far enough to give him the grape right into his lips. I wonder now why I could not have perceived at once that calm gentleness; in all the hundreds of times I have fed them, putting my fingers right between their lips, neither has ever tried to bite me or to snatch."

From that time on, Belle became their special friend. Only once was she frightened, and then it turned out that the gorilla was more frightened than she.

She was feeding the two of them when she dropped a grape into the cage. She leaned forward to pick it up in order to give it to Ngagi. But apparently Ngagi thought she was taking it away, because he grabbed her arm with his enormous black hand. Belle was wearing a blue sweater. She let it slip down her arm, and as Ngagi kept pulling, she unbuttoned the sweater, letting it slide off her arm and into the cage.

"When he saw that I was white where before I had been blue, he was terror-stricken and shoved the sweater back at me through the bars. Then he went to the farther corner, where he watched me sullenly from under lowered brows until I put the sweater back on."

Mbongo had allowed Belle to touch him, to stroke his huge arms and thick fur, but the older Ngagi had not. One day, when she was playing with Mbongo, Ngagi came near them, edging a little closer every few minutes. She gently touched Ngagi's arm, but the gorilla pulled away. The second time he allowed her to touch, but he would not look at her. He turned his head.

"He was very tense," said Belle. "I rubbed my hand firmly down the great arm, then across the shoulders. For the first time I really took hold of his arm, closing my fingers tightly around it. I spoke softly but firmly, just saying his name. To tell the truth, I was so excited that my voice was very husky, and I felt as though my tongue were much too thick. Hearing my voice, he turned his face directly toward me and looked straight into my eyes. Then he heaved a great sigh and relaxed against the steel bars of the sleeping room. His big, black face was covered with great beads of sweat, and I realized how much greater had been his victory than mine and how difficult it had been to overcome his reluctance to human touch. Mine was the first contact the great gorilla had ever received without fear and resentment."

Belle observed visiting scientists who came to San Diego to study the gorillas, and she learned something about interpreting some of the animals' actions and activities. But the more she watched, the more she believed that the ability to judge the intelligence of any wild creature depends very much on the intelligence of the person doing the watching. And she firmly believed that it was not right to make any statement about the intelligence of a whole group of animals just from watching one or two of those animals in a zoo. It is never fair to judge a group by the actions of a few individuals.

The more she knew about the gorillas, chimpanzees, and orangutans in the zoo, the more she hoped that someone would go into the wild someday and find out what those animals were really like.

Even though she hoped for those studies in the wild, she loved the zoo, and she was certain that it had an important place in the civilized world.

"I have come to scorn the theory of some people," she said, "who believe that everything can be learned in the wild and who, therefore, dislike zoos. Where could they go and in the course of the morning watch a snake shed its skin, a young parrot learn to fly, and a newborn fawn "freeze" at the command of its young mother? Have they ever seen even one of these things happen in the wild? Probably not, but I have seen all of them in the zoo."

Belle called herself an "armchair" naturalist because what she learned about animals came from reading books and watching in the zoo.

Only a few times did she go on collecting expeditions. On the first trip, she was not a representative of the zoo or even one of the collectors, but only a chaperone. A group of men had chartered a boat to go into the Pacific in search of some rare Guadalupe fur seals that were almost extinct because so many had been hunted. A young woman who had been on an earlier voyage volunteered to go along as a guide. She said she knew exactly where to find the seals.

But the ship's captain was horrified at the idea of a woman traveling with so many men without a chaperone. So Belle was appointed the young lady's official guardian. Unfortunately, they did not see a single fur seal on that trip.

Belle retired from the San Diego Zoo in December 1953, after twenty-eight years. Under her care, the collection had grown to 3,500 animals, including the only three koala bears outside of Australia. They thrived because their only food—the leaves of the eucalyptus tree—grew there. The zoo became famous for the great number of baby animals born and raised there, many of them rare. And the collection of semitropical plants that grew on the grounds became as famous as the animals.

The gigantic flight cages built against the canyon walls so that eagles, hawks, and other birds of prey could soar on the wind currents were Belle's idea. She taught herself to become an expert on animal enclosures, giving each animal room enough to enjoy life, but not allowing escape routes. She was generous with her help, and many small zoos all over North America grew because of her ideas.

Just about every schoolchild in San Diego knew Belle Benchley as the "zoo lady." She was never too busy to stop at an animal's enclosure to tell people some special story. She cared for the people who worked with the animals, too. She was never too busy to learn, and in turn she taught others about the animals in her man-made jungle. She was a good zoo keeper.

Chapter Three
Ruth Harkness and the *Bei-Shung*

Five people slipped and scrambled over snow-covered boulders, through the wet, muddy gullies of the high Himalaya mountains. The thirty-degree temperature and constant drizzle of snow and rain soaked through their clothes and chilled them.

First in line was a tall, twenty-year-old Chinese guide. He was followed closely by two porters—men from a nearby village, carrying food and camp equipment. Next, falling and often crawling on her hands and knees, came a young American woman. An ancient-looking Tibetan hunter, whose many layers of ragged clothes looked as though he had never been out of them, stayed close behind the woman, boosting her along if she needed help.

They were on the last leg of a thirty-day journey that had taken them 1,500 miles up the Yangtze River from Shanghai, first by steamer and then by junk. After that, they rode on rickety trucks, and one day they traveled in wheelbarrows. But most often they walked to the Szechuan Province, near Tibet. It was 1936, and they were in search of the *bei-shung,* the giant panda, an animal no one had ever seen alive outside of China.

The giant panda is an animal like no other. It looks like a black and white bear. It is slow and clumsy and not very bright, but it has no need for speed or agility or intelligence. It lives in the dense bamboo thickets of the high Himalaya, where it does not need to hurry or outwit predators. It shares the territory with the snow leopard, an animal that might help itself to a baby giant panda but would be unlikely to attack a full-grown one.

What we do know about pandas comes from dissecting dead ones or watching them in zoos. No field studies have been made. No zoologist has settled into the bamboo thickets to spend a season, shivering and wet, just hoping to get a glimpse of this animal that travels alone.

In 1869, when the giant panda was first described scientifically, a battle began among scientists as to what other animals the panda is related to. That battle continues to this day.

One group of biologists is certain that pandas have evolved from the bears, and another group of equally well trained scientists claim that the panda is really a member of the racoon family. Each group bases its conclusions on the panda's anatomy—comparing the teeth, or the shape of the brain, or the sex organs, or the way it digests its food, to other animals. But recently, Chinese zoologists and American scientists from the Smithsonian Institution reported that a panda is a panda.

Its scientific name is *Ailuropoda melanoleuca,* which means "black and white cat-footed animal." And if you watch the giant panda in the zoo, you will be surprised at how catlike its footing is as it climbs and tumbles, even though it looks like a clumsy bear.

One biologist calls the panda's head a "crunching machine" because it is a heavy skull with broad, strong jaws and teeth like grinding stumps for chewing stalks of bamboo.

On each of the panda's front feet is a sixth claw, which is really not a claw at all. It is a wrist bone covered with a fleshy pad that has evolved as a kind of thumb. Although it is placed where a human's little finger would be, it works like a human's thumb. This enables a panda to grasp things. There is a very human look to a panda when it eats, because it always carries food to its mouth instead of lowering its head to the food.

From the time the panda was known outside of China, in 1869, it became the supreme challenge for big-game hunters. Everyone wanted to get one. A few museums had skins or bones, but those had been purchased from the Chinese.

In 1928, Colonel Theodore Roosevelt and Kermit Roosevelt, sons of American President Teddy Roosevelt, went on a highly publicized expedition for the Field Museum in Chicago. They killed a giant panda, and its skin was mounted for an exhibit.

William Harkness was an explorer and animal collector. In 1934, he returned from an Asian expedition on which he captured the giant Komodo dragons for the Bronx Zoo. He was already planning his next trip and telling his fiancée, Ruth McCombs, about it.

"I'm going to Tibet after a giant panda," he told Ruth.

"Giant panther, don't you mean?" asked Ruth.

As Bill told her more about the animal and the trip, Ruth became more and more excited. She asked if she could go.

"No," he told her. "Not that a woman couldn't make herself useful, but governments make such a fuss if anything happens to a woman."

In September 1934, Ruth and Bill Harkness were married. Two weeks later, Bill sailed on the panda expedition.

"There was nothing I could do but wait patiently," said Ruth. She stayed in New York City and continued working as a dress designer.

It took the Harkness expedition until January to reach Shanghai. By that time, three of the four men in the group had dropped out. They had had trouble at every turn. Time dragged as Bill, trying to continue alone, failed to get permission to go into the interior of China.

And then one day, with no warning, Ruth received a cable telling her that her husband had died of some strange disease in Shanghai.

"I had inherited an expedition," she wrote later.

Knowing nothing about either expeditions or pandas, but feeling it was absolutely the right thing to do, Ruth Harkness set out alone on the long journey in April. There were no planes, no fast jets in those days. A slow ship crossed the Atlantic, sailed through the Mediterranean and the Red Sea, around India, and finally to Shanghai.

There she spent months settling her husband's affairs, a tangle of accounts and equipment. And all the while she listened to talk of the civil war that raged in China, the tales of the Red Army that moved relentlessly, the bandits who preyed upon travelers, and the dangers for a foreign woman alone. But she also listened to exciting stories of the animals that lived in the snow-capped mountains.

No one encouraged her. She was simply told that if she did not die of dysentery or some other disease, she would surely be shot by the bandits. The Chinese newspapers began to call her the "foreign devil." But she stubbornly refused to go back.

All that long summer she sweltered in Shanghai, looking, she said, "rather like a second-rate steamed clam." There was no air conditioning. She waited for fall because she hoped the pandas might move to lower altitudes.

She knew that the animals lived from six to twelve thousand feet up the mountainsides, and she reasoned that they might come down to find fresh bamboo in September, when the snow began to cover the foliage higher up the slopes.

"Being a naturally lazy person," she said, "I could see no reason for climbing up to meet them if there was a probability of their coming down to meet me."

While she waited, she organized the equipment. And she fell in love with China. "There was a curious feeling in me that this was not an alien land, a strange and foreign country, but in some inexplicable way . . . home."

She met a young guide, Quentin Young, whose older brother had shown the Roosevelt brothers through panda country. She hired him, and together they made plans.

Authorities told Ruth to apply for a permit for a scientific expedition, but she did not do it. Her husband had not been able to get such a permit, and she did not expect that she would have any better luck. "Besides," she said, "I thought that certainly doesn't affect me because I'm not a scientist, certainly not a zoologist, just a designer of dresses who had, according to my friends, gone haywire."

And so she put aside the idea of trying to get official help.

She and Quentin went to the warehouse where the equipment from her husband's expedition was stored. They sorted through box after box of guns and ammunition, clothing, boots, tents, cots, and medicine. It was an enormous job just trying to decide what they would need for months of living in the mountains.

But even more difficult was selecting what equipment to take for capturing the panda. How do you trap a giant panda? How big is one? How dangerous? Just to be safe, they decided to take bales of wire, coils of strong rope, and five big traps that could hold a three- or four-hundred-pound animal without harming it.

One night after a long session of list-making, Ruth was lying in bed, wondering how on earth they would ever carry an animal that size down a mountain. And suddenly she thought, "Why not get a baby one?"

"I got out of bed and made a shopping note on my memo pad," she wrote later. "Nursing bottle, nipples, dried milk."

Finally, in September of 1936, just two years after her husband had started his expedition, Ruth Harkness began the most difficult part of the journey to the border of Tibet.

One day, after the long boat trips and truck rides, the group stopped to rest at a ruined temple at a mountain pass. As they sat on the hard-packed dirt floor drinking tea, Ruth listened to the porters talking about the *bei-shung,* the ferocious animal that would leap at you from fifteen feet away, the beast that could bite off a dog's leg as quickly as you could blink.

Ruth was excited rather than frightened by the thought that she would really see a giant panda. She was never sure she could capture one, but she knew she would stay in the mountains at least until she saw the *bei-shung.*

The next day, leaving most of the equipment and all but two of the porters in a village, Quentin, Ruth, and the old hunter, Tsang, continued up the mountains. They carried little more than toothbrushes and sleeping bags. The other porters were given instructions to follow later with enough equipment to set up a mountain base camp.

For eight days they climbed over slippery boulders, down steep crevasses to the river bed, up even higher slopes. The swaying rope bridges across the deep ravines were scary. It took all the courage Ruth had to make herself cross them. Once they met an old herb digger and asked him if he had seen a panda. *"Bei-shung,"* he moaned, and muttered something about a *bei-shung* as big as a horse that had chewed his iron cooking pot.

One day they traveled thirty miles, scrambling, sliding, falling, until they found a spot that Quentin thought would make a good base camp. Snow fell, adding a silent beauty that made everything seem unreal.

When the porters with the tents finally arrived and the base camp was set up, Ruth settled down to enjoy the luxury of a tent overhead, a place to change clothes, a cot to stretch out on, and food cooked in a pot over a big fire. She hoped to have a month or more to catch up on her writing in the journal she was keeping and to explore the country. Quentin went on to set up a second camp, higher up the slopes.

Just a day or two after moving into the base camp, Ruth was pounding dirty socks on rocks in ancient laundry fashion when she heard shouts and signal shots. Quentin had returned from Camp 2. He raced toward her yelling, *"Bei-shung, bei-shung!"*

"Did you see one? Catch one?" she called as she ran toward him.

When Quentin caught his breath, he explained that they had seen signs of the giant panda—fresh dung and claw marks on bamboo.

The next morning at dawn, November 9, Ruth and Quentin followed the hunter, Tsang, and the two porters toward Camp 2 to inspect the traps.

The climb through the bamboo thickets to the second camp made the first part of the trip seem as easy as a walk on a paved road.

Bamboo had fallen in places, creating slimy wet traps into which the group fell up to their waists. Branches caught at boot laces and buttons so that it took every ounce of strength to pull out. Most of the time they crawled on their hands and knees.

Suddenly there was the sound of a shot ahead. Ruth tried to run, but she only slipped and fell more than before.

"What is it?" she yelled.

"*Bei-shung,*" Quentin's voice echoed through the mountains.

Ruth was furious. She had given strict orders that there was to be no shooting in trapping areas. She stopped to listen. Silence. Only the dripping of water from leaves. They moved on toward a group of larger trees that stood in an area where the bamboo thickets were not so dense.

Near the trees they stopped again to listen. Suddenly Quentin charged ahead. "I couldn't keep up with him," said Ruth. "I could see him dimly through the wet branches. I stumbled blindly, brushing water from my face and eyes. Then I stopped, frozen in my tracks. From the old dead tree came a baby's whimper."

"Listen," she called, but Quentin already was thrusting his long arms into the hollow of the tree. He pulled out a fuzzy black and white ball and held it out to her.

"I reached for the tiny thing, a squirming, baby *bei-shung* . . . not a fantasy."

The woolly ball nuzzled her jacket as though looking for a place to nurse.

"It's hungry," she said.

Without another word, both she and Quentin hurried toward camp and the nursing bottle and dried milk that were packed away. The climb that had taken them five weary hours seemed like no time at all on the way back to base camp.

Quentin took the baby from Ruth and tucked it between the two warm shirts he was wearing, cradling the tiny animal safely in one arm. Ruth slid down the mountain. "In my determination to keep up with Quentin, I forgot to be a sissy on the bridges and went unhesitatingly across them. The baby was hungry!" she said.

From that moment on, every concern was for the baby giant panda.

It had to survive. It weighed three pounds, and its eyes were still closed. Ruth named it Su Lin, which means "a little bit of something very cute."

Ruth never did find out what happened to the baby's mother. Had it been shot? The guides searched the bamboo thickets but did not find her.

Back in the tent, Ruth rocked the baby in her arms as Quentin mixed and warmed the milk. After a few fussy moments, Su Lin took to the bottle hungrily, as though she had always been fed from a bottle. While the baby was eating, porters from the village arrived with the additional equipment that Quentin had ordered at the last minute— heavy tongs "for holding down a struggling panda," a stout collar, chains, and a padlock.

Before they packed to return to Shanghai with the baby, Ruth sent a porter out to bring back some bamboo trees. She wanted to be sure that whatever scientific society raised the baby would also know something of the food it ate.

For the next three months, Ruth did not have a whole night's sleep. Like any new mother, she had a baby to feed, and that baby let her know when it was hungry.

All the way back to Shanghai, they avoided the inns they had used on the way up the mountain. One night they found an empty shelter, a bare room with a sand floor. They shared it with the four porters, four hunters, the baby panda, and a pony. They wanted to keep Su Lin away from too many prying eyes. Ruth found her biggest problem was keeping the baby from being cuddled to death.

As they hurried back to Shanghai, Ruth wondered what the trip from camp out of the mountains would have been like if the panda had been a three- or four-hundred-pound adult instead of a three-pound infant.

In her notes she wrote, "A struggling animal, carried in a cage, miserable and made frantic by crowds of curious people; I don't think, even if it could have been managed, I would have had the heart to go through with it."

The problems of climbing mountains and finding the panda were nothing compared to the problems Ruth faced when she tried to

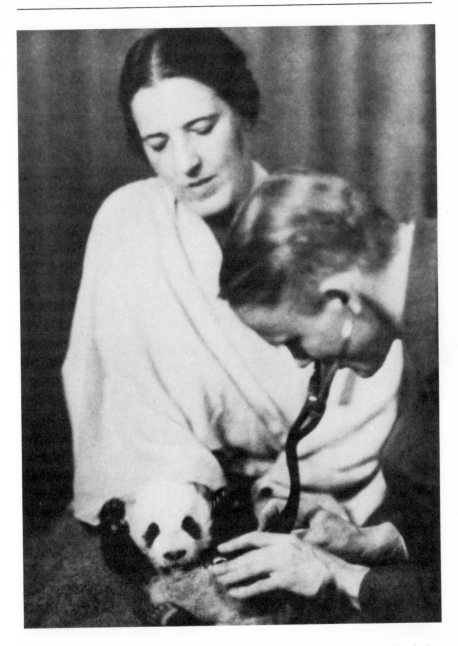

Ruth Harkness had a doctor in Shanghai check Su Lin when the baby panda had a stomach ache. The doctor had never heard of a panda. (J. B. Lippincott)

take Su Lin out of China. She had broken all the rules: a scientific expedition without permission from the Chinese government—an expedition, she told someone, "that in my wildest dreams I had never thought would be successful."

Ruth stayed in a hotel with Su Lin, leaving windows open to keep the baby comfortable. One evening Su Lin took her bottle too quickly, and Ruth paced the floor with the whimpering animal as a mother would with a colicky baby. She called a baby doctor in Shanghai, and he said he could come immediately, "but what the devil is a baby pandor?"

After all sorts of problems, including a shipping strike that kept them in Shanghai for sixteen days, they were ready to sail. At the last moment they were stopped by customs, and Ruth spent an uncomfortable night in the customs offices. Finally, with the payment of two dollars for a permit, Ruth was allowed to sail on the U.S.S. *President McKinley*. The animal was listed in the passenger voucher as "one dog."

Just before Christmas of 1936, the ship docked in San Francisco. Even then there were problems when reservations on a cross-country train were mixed up. A wild cab ride with the baby panda across the city to the train station seemed almost too much for Ruth, but they caught the train to Chicago and then New York.

For reasons that are not clear, the Bronx Zoo, which had sent William Harkness on the first expedition, was not interested in the giant panda. Perhaps they were worried about what to feed the tiny animal.

Ruth was invited to the all-male Explorers Club in New York, the first exception to their all-male rule. It was their thirty-third annual banquet, and Ruth and Su Lin received a standing ovation.

The Roosevelt brothers who had shot a panda years earlier told Ruth that after seeing Su Lin, they could never shoot another. In that way, Su Lin helped to take some of the glamour from the era of big-game hunting. After all, when a woman can go into the highest mountains and bring home a furry baby animal, it does not seem quite so brave for a group of men to go to the same place armed with guns to bring out a dead animal.

Finally, in February 1937, Su Lin went to live at the Brookfield Zoo in Chicago. After a two-month separation, Ruth returned to see her.

"I wasn't quite prepared for the Su Lin who the first time I had ever held her just filled the hollow of my two hands," said Ruth. The baby had grown into a big bearlike animal.

"When I called her name, she rolled over slowly and looked at me. I drew nearer, and suddenly she was up and over the side of her pen and lunging into my arms. She buried her nose in my hair as she had done when she had slept with me, and slobbered over my ear."

Although Su Lin remained in Chicago, Ruth was not content to stay in a city. "Again there were visions of blue seas, high mountains, and the beauty of that far lonely country," she said.

Ruth returned to Tibet a second time. She brought back another young panda, Diana, as a companion for Su Lin. But Su Lin died in the spring of 1938, when a splinter of wood stuck in her throat. A third trip to panda country followed, and Ruth brought out a third panda. But this time her attitude changed considerably.

The third little panda could not seem to settle down to a captive life, no matter what Ruth did to make it content. "It seemed obvious to me," she said, "that an unhappy baby animal could be of no value scientifically."

All Ruth had to show for her care were scratches and infections. "And if an animal does not like me," she said, "it gives me a far greater sense of inferiority than if a human being does not."

So she put the expedition into reverse. She and her cook, Wang, traveled back into the bamboo jungle to leave Su Sen, the third panda, in exactly the same spot where it had been captured. They lived nearby in a cave for a week, waiting for the young panda to come back for the food they had been feeding her. But days and nights went by, and she did not return. Finally, they did see the panda, but Ruth thinks it was by mistake that the little animal happened by the cave. She said, "The little black and white furry youngster looked just once at civilization in the form of Wang and me and ran as though the demons of hell were at her heels."

Although Ruth brought the first panda out of China alive, making it the most famous animal in the twentieth century, she was the subject of many newspaper articles in which reporters questioned her honesty. How had she been able to find the young of an animal as elusive as the giant panda? She did not deny the help she had from guides and hunters in Tibet. Some thought that perhaps villagers had shot adult pandas and sold the orphaned animals to her. No one will ever know for sure. But considering the incredible feat of making such expeditions and even keeping such babies alive during the long journeys from the mountains and back to America, Ruth Harkness deserves rightful praise and respect.

Today, many zoos have pandas. The Chinese government now protects the panda in its natural habitat, and they have bred them successfully in their fine zoos. They raise the young on the natural bamboo and other foods from the animals' homeland.

But it was Ruth Harkness, with her sense of adventure and her consuming desire to find this unknown animal, who let the world know the panda as something more than a hunter's trophy.

Chapter Four

Jane Goodall and
the Community of Chimpanzees

A white-bearded chimpanzee squatted next to the red-dirt mound of a termite nest. With a look of intense concentration, he poked a long blade of sword grass into a hole in the nest. He pulled it out slowly and picked off the insects that clung to it. When the grass was bent, he threw it away. Reaching out to some vines growing nearby, he picked another stick, and with a quick stroke of his hand, he stripped the leaves off. He bit off one end of this newly made tool, wet it with his lips, and poked it into the hole again to fish for food.

About sixty yards away, only partly hidden in the tall, wet grass, a slender young blonde woman watched through binoculars for more than an hour as this chimpanzee snacked on termites. She recognized the large male chimpanzee as the one she called David Greybeard. When he wandered off, Jane Goodall hurried to the termite mound and poked a stick into the hole. She pulled it out and tasted one of the insects that hung onto the stick—just as she has tasted most everything she has seen the chimpanzees eat.

Jane Goodall had been watching the chimpanzees in the Gombe Stream Game Reserve on the shores of Lake Tanganyika in Africa for four months when she saw the chimpanzee make tools. For eight days she hurried to the same spot at dawn to watch. On the eighth day she saw other chimps scratch open sealed-over holes in the nests and poke grass or stick tools in for food. This was an exciting discovery, and it made all the lonely hours of watching, the bruised legs, and the mosquito bites matter not a bit. Until this time, man was considered to be the only toolmaker. This was the first recorded instance of an animal taking a natural object and changing it in some way so that it could be used as a tool.

Later she discovered this same group of animals making sponges to scoop up water from hollow logs or small places that they could not reach with their mouths. They chewed leaves just enough to crush them, put the leaf sponge into the water to soak it up, and sucked on the green sponge. When she tried it, she found she could get a lot more water with the crushed leaves than with leaves fresh from a tree. The chimps used leaves as napkins to wipe messy babies or blood that dripped from a piece of meat.

Other animals *use* tools. The sea otter takes a stone from the ocean bottom, places it on its chest, and uses it to crack open abalone shells. Some birds use sticks to poke into holes to find grubs and insects. But the *making* of tools was such an important discovery that Jane Goodall wired the news to Dr. Louis Leakey, the scientist who made it possible for her to go to Tanzania in 1960 to study the chimpanzees.

Today Jane Goodall is almost a legend. There have been several television specials about her work in Gombe, and she has lectured in many cities. She has conducted the longest single study of primates in their natural habitat. When she began, she knew nothing about chimpanzees, and she believes that may be one reason she was chosen to do such important work.

From the time she was eight years old, she knew she would some-day live in Africa among the wild animals. Her constant companion was, oddly enough, a toy chimpanzee. In her home town of Bourne-mouth, England, there weren't many wild animals, but she liked to watch the chickens, and she read about animals all the time. After high school, she took a secretarial course and worked at jobs that had nothing to do with animal studies. But she never gave up her dream of going to Africa.

When an invitation came in 1960 to visit friends in Kenya, Africa, she immediately quit her job in London. Living expenses were high in the city, and it would have been difficult to save money there. So she went home to Bournemouth and spent the summer working as a waitress until she had saved the fare to Africa.

A month after she arrived in Africa, she took a friend's suggestion and called on Dr. Leakey, who was then a curator at the natural his-tory museum in Nairobi.

"I had never heard of him," she told an audience years later, "and I was rather shy, but I contacted him."

Dr. Leakey was an anthropologist who was searching for the skeletal remains of early man. Jane talked with him for a while, and he offered her a job at the museum. She accepted.

"It was exciting to work for such a dynamic man," she said. "He had tremendous impact on all of his students."

Dr. Leakey invited Jane to go with him and his wife, Mary, on one of their expeditions to Olduvai Gorge on the Serengeti Plains in Tanzania. They worked long hours in the hot sun each day, sifting and sorting through dirt, looking for bone fragments, tools, broken bits of any small thing that might be a clue to the life of early man.

In the evenings, Dr. Leakey talked to Jane about the chimpanzee, an animal found only in Africa along the equatorial forest regions. He told her he was interested in learning about the behavior of a group of chimpanzees living along a lake shore because the remains of early man were often found along such shores. He believed some-thing could be learned about the behavior of early man by studying primates living in similar conditions.

When Dr. Leakey asked Jane if she would like to try such a study, she could hardly believe it. "I had no qualifications at all," she said. "But I believe he knew that my interest in animals was not just a passing phase."

Dr. Leakey assured Jane that he wanted someone with patience and understanding, and without a mind full of scientific theories. He wanted someone who would study chimpanzees for no reason other than the desire to know about them.

Money, unfortunately, is always a problem in any scientific research. Someone has to pay the bills. So while Jane waited for Dr. Leakey to find a sponsor for the chimpanzee study, she returned to England to learn what she could about the animals with whom she would be sharing her life.

Pan satyrus is the scientific name for the long-haired or eastern chimpanzee that Jane would be watching. It is an ape, not a monkey. The anthropoid, or manlike, apes are the gibbon, orangutan, chimpanzee, and gorilla. They have no tails, and instead of a big toe on each foot they have a thumb. The ape can use both its hands and feet as man uses his two hands.

The chimpanzees are large animals, covered with coarse black or brown hair except on their hands, feet, and face. A male may stand five feet tall and weigh 100 to 120 pounds. Although they live together in communities numbering thirty to forty, they are difficult to watch in the wild because they roam around their home territory of some thirty square miles, feeding in trees and making nests wherever they happen to be at dusk. The large groups gather when rich supplies of food are found. Only the mothers and their young travel together all the time.

When Jane finally received word that money had been found to support a six-month study, she was anxious to get started. The first setback came when she was told that African officials would not allow her to live in the reserve without a companion. They could not understand why anyone would want to travel all the way from England just to look at apes anyway. And they certainly were not going to allow her to put herself in danger. Jane's mother, Vanne Goodall, agreed to stay with her, and that satisfied the officials. Then they insisted on assigning game scouts to stay with her. One man told her later he expected her to pack up and leave within six weeks.

When camp had been set up the first night in a clearing not far from the beach, Jane went off by herself. She climbed the lower slope of the mountain, made slippery by a recent fire that burned off the tall grass. That night she took her camp cot from the tent and slept under the stars. She felt at home.

The first few weeks were difficult. Not only was it hard to see the black animals through the trees, but wherever Jane went the game scouts were not far off. She wanted only to be alone, to allow the chimpanzees to get used to this hairless, light-colored ape in khaki covering. She wore dark green or khaki clothes so she would blend with the vegetation and not startle the chimps.

Several times she saw the animals feeding close to her, but as soon as they spotted her, they vanished into the forest. Finally, the game scouts left when they realized she really was going into the forest every day and not just counting chimps from a boat in the lake. She wanted to be near the chimp nesting site when the animals awoke, so she had a piece of bread and a cup of coffee and set out by five-thirty as the sun was breaking over the mountains.

"Because I always stationed myself in the same place and never crept up to them or appeared unexpectedly, the chimps at last began to accept me," she explained.

For a while all the chimps looked alike, but as she watched, Jane began to see individual differences. She gave them names that seemed to suit them. Other scientists give animals numbers. They think names are anthropomorphic. But Jane wanted to emphasize the individuals, to get to know them as intimately as possible.

David Greybeard, with his white beard and his calm, gentle disposition, was the first to allow her to approach closely without running away. She had been at Gombe eight months when one day she came upon some chimps. "I got much closer to the group than I had planned," she said. "My jungle lore was rather poor, and to my amazement they just sat there . . . three of them: David Greybeard, Goliath, and one female. They watched me, they stared, and they went on grooming. I'll never forget that. It was the first moment of acceptance."

Getting an animal accustomed to humans is called habituating. "I think that the process of habituation would have happened without David Greybeard; he just hastened it tremendously. When I would meet the chimps out in the forest, David wouldn't run away. He was a very calm chimp. He had tremendous qualities of leadership, primarily because he was gentle, and the other chimps would follow him."

Flo was an old female, easily recognized by her large, bulbous nose and raggedy ears. She was not a handsome animal, but the other chimps seemed fond of her. When Jane first saw her, Flo was carrying her baby daughter, Fifi, on her back; her six-year-old son, Figan, was with her, too. It was Flo's family that taught Jane most about the family life of these animals.

Every day she took notes, not trusting to memory all the little things that might be important. "I recorded everything I saw, no matter how insignificant it seemed," she said.

At night, back at camp, she bathed in a small canvas tub, had supper by campfire, and sat up rewriting her notes long after midnight by the light of kerosene lamps.

The notes began to add up to an enormous amount of information. Not only had Jane discovered the toolmaking of the chimps, but she made another important discovery as well. She found that chimps are carnivorous—that they eat meat. No one had seen the animals kill for food, but she had observed them in organized, efficient hunts for baby baboons, young bushbuck, and several kinds of monkeys.

She collected and tasted most of the two hundred different foods the chimps eat, including ants, termites, grubs, fruit, blossoms, seeds, bark, leaves, and even the dead fiber of some trees. Occasionally she saw them take eggs or fledgling birds from their nests.

A young chimpanzee has much to learn. He is born as helpless as a newborn human, and his mother cradles him in her arm, carrying him wherever she goes. The infant nurses for about three minutes every hour and continues to nurse until he is five or six years old. When the mother stops cradling the child constantly and puts it down now and then, the child has to learn to answer to her signals. At first, when the mother is ready to move on, she reaches out and picks the baby up. Later, the child learns to respond just to the touch of her hand. At five or six weeks, the baby begins to ride on the mother's back.

A young wild chimpanzee named Figan clasps hands with Dr. Jane Goodall, a reward for her five years of patience and courage studying chimps in the African wilds. (Photo by Baron Hugo van Lawick, © National Geographic Society)

The first chimp baby that Jane watched learning to walk was six months old, and he worried her. He staggered and was so clumsy that she thought there must be something terribly wrong. In the years that followed, she was to see many youngsters do the same thing. She has now seen second and third generations, and she knows that they have a long, slow development.

The Gombe Stream Research Station and the chimp studies had a long, slow development, too. Jane's mother stayed with her less than a year. Graduate students from various universities joined her for short periods to study the plants or insects of the region, and many came to learn from Jane how to watch the chimps. Dr. Leakey sent a young Dutch photographer, Hugo van Lawick, to record Jane's chimp community. In 1964 Jane and Hugo were married, and they continued the studies together for several years.

The question most asked of Dr. Jane Goodall (who now has a Ph.D. from Oxford University in animal behavior) is, "Why have you studied chimpanzees all these years? Surely you must have all the answers by now."

Jane is quick to answer. "It wasn't until we'd been at Gombe thirteen years that we began to understand anything about the nature of communities."

In the beginning she noticed general things, such as what the chimps ate, how they made their nests, how they spent their days, and how they communicated with each other. They have a large vocabulary of calls. There are sounds for fear, pain, pleasure, and what Jane calls "food-barks." They laugh, very much like humans, and they love to play. There is also a communication based on touch.

Chimpanzees are very social animals. They enjoy being with each other. When they meet, they greet each other with kisses, hugs, pats on the back, and hand-holding. Grooming—the gentle parting of the hair, combing, and touching—is an important social function. It is peaceful, relaxing, friendly physical contact.

There is a definite social order among the chimpanzees, with a leader in each community. Scientists call the leader the alpha male. Not every male tries for this position. Some seem quite content to be followers. But those who do contend for the alpha position work hard to get to the top.

In 1962, when Jane had been at Gombe for two years, Goliath was the alpha male. He made magnificent displays of power when the group met—sort of reminders that he was the leader. He waved branches, panted and hooted, hit trees, and generally made a big noise.

Jane started the "banana club" in order to watch individuals more closely. She had bananas shipped in and made them available to the animals. The chimps came into camp, sometimes into her tent, to get them. But she did not make pets of the animals. They were always wild, even though she got to know them well.

At that time another male, Mike, had quite a low position in the group. Almost every other male attacked him. But he watched carefully and eventually began his campaign to get ahead. Kerosene was used for fuel in camp, and there were several empty kerosene cans lying around. Mike was the only chimp in the area intelligent enough to make use of them. At first he kicked one can along the ground. It made a wonderful banging that sent the other chimps running. Then he used two, deliberately aiming them at a group of males that were quietly feeding. In just four months Mike became the alpha male without a single fight. When Jane could no longer stand the racket of Mike's displays, she took the cans away. But Mike found buckets, camp chairs, anything not fastened down as substitutes. When he could find nothing else, he made do with rocks and sticks. For six years he was the alpha male.

One of the things the long study showed is the strong bond of affection between mothers and their young, and between brothers. Brothers seem to remain friends for life and are always helping each other.

Years after Mike waged his dramatic campaign for leadership, Figan, one of Flo's older sons, gave it a try. He was a small male, but he really seemed to want to be the alpha male. He made good use of his brother Fabin. They traveled everywhere together, and they displayed and charged only when they were together. Figan was always in control. He planned the displays. Jane observed him as he watched the group from a high spot of ground. He would survey things for a while, then walk silently to get into position. Then he would come sweeping down with loud cries, waving branches, with brother Fabin adding to the noise. Figan has been alpha male for some years now, and those working at the Gombe Stream Research Station are guessing who will be next.

The father does not play a role in family life. In fact, it is seldom known which males father which infants within the group. But all males defend all infants. Males play with the children, allowing them to crawl all over them. They tickle them, pat them on the head, and chuck them under the chin. The strongest bond is between mothers and sons.

Just a few months before she died, old Flo heard her son Figan scream. Flo began to run toward him. Figan was twenty-one or twenty-two years old at the time. He had gotten into a fight and had fallen from a tree, hurting his wrist. There was nothing Flo could do, but she calmed him, touching him gently. He went off with her, and Flo stayed with him until his wrist had healed and he was able to fend for himself again.

"We firmly believe that a complete understanding of the social activities of the chimpanzee will prove of inestimable value to better assessment of much of our own human behavior," said Jane. She also believes that much can be learned from the chimps about child-rearing and adolescence. "I am not necessarily saying that we should do as the chimps do, but we certainly have room for improvement."

Because Jane admired the patient, gentle way that old Flo and the other female chimps raised their children, she copied some of the same ideas when she had her son, Hugo Junior, whom they nick-named "Grub," in 1967. For example, she would gently distract him from an activity she did not want him to do and show him something else to play with. She also employed constant contact and touching which is an important part of chimp child-rearing, too.

There are many similarities between man and chimp—gestures, expression, the use of tools which is traditional but changes from one community to another, the joy of play that continues into the adult years, and another similarity which is now being studied—aggression.

Today at the Gombe Research Station, graduate students are observing two communities of chimps. They have watched small patrols of chimps go to the edge of their territory, walking in close groups, traveling in silence. The chimps keep long watches, looking into the valley for as long as an hour at a time. They have attacked and killed chimps from the bordering territory.

"This is something we never would have learned about if we'd given up studying chimps. And we still don't know why they do it," Jane told an audience.

They have seen cannibalism, too—a group of chimps attacking an adult female from another community and eating the baby. Only the years of study ahead will tell why. Is it because their territory is too crowded now? Is it because neighboring villages are creeping too close to their forest and man is invading, if only to find firewood?

Jane's life has changed considerably since 1960, when she first went into the African rain forest. She is now a visiting professor at Stanford University and an active participant in the L. S. B. Leakey Foundation, with many graduate students studying her techniques of animal watching. She divorced Hugo van Lawick some years ago and is married now to Derek Bryceson, the director of Tanzania's nine national parks and the only elected white person in black African government. Because of unrest in the African nations, Jane can no longer live at the Gombe Research Station, which has grown from a tent near the shore of Lake Tanganyika to a series of low buildings where her graduate students live and study. Tanzanian students run the station now, and Jane keeps in touch, returning there every five or six weeks. She travels and lectures to raise money to keep the study going.

One of her happiest memories is of the day she followed David Greybeard back into the mountains. "I had the feeling that David almost appreciated my company, for several times he waited while I scrambled after him through some tangle of vegetation."

David rested now and then, and they drank side by side from a clear mountain stream. Jane saw a red palm nut on the ground. She held it out to David. He looked at it but turned away. "Then, as I held it nearer, he deliberately reached out, laid his hand over mine, and taking the nut between his thumb and palm he gently squeezed my hand. It was at least ten seconds before he released my hand from his firm warm clasp."

So the study at Gombe goes on. "We have just about got to the stage of knowing which questions to ask," Jane Goodall says thoughtfully.

Chapter Five

Kay McKeever and a Parliament of Owls

Tiglet is a screech owl not much bigger than a fat robin. His favorite perch is the top shelf of a bookcase in Kay McKeever's living room. There he waits until Morag, an enormous Irish wolfhound, has settled in to sleep on the rug. Then, without a sound, Tiglet swoops from the top shelf with his talons ready. Barely hesitating in flight, he rakes Morag's curly backside with his long claws. Before the gangly dog can scramble to his feet, Tiglet has swooped back again and is peacefully perched on the shelf as though nothing had happened.

Tiglet spends the daylight hours confined to a large bathroom. After the McKeevers' dinner, Tiglet is allowed the freedom of the house, flying wherever he pleases. At bedtime, Kay calls him with a screech owl call. Tiglet flies to her head, and she carries him back to his bathroom where his dinner—a freshly thawed dead mouse— lies neatly on a paper towel next to the sink.

As the moon rises over the tall pines that surround the McKeevers' house in Vineland, Ontario, you can hear the chorus of soft, haunting hoots mixed with a dozen other screeches, sighs, and cries as one hundred owls settle in for the night.

The owls live in large, outdoor flight cages at the Owl Research and Rehabilitation Center—the only one of its kind in North America. Tiglet, and a great horned owl named Wheeper, are the only ones who don't seem to know they are owls.

Tiglet and Wheeper have been imprinted with humans. Imprinting is nature's method of making sure a baby animal will know its mother. When a baby duck or goose hatches from the egg, the first moving, living thing it sees becomes imprinted on it as the parent, the source of food. A baby goose will follow the farmer if that is who it has seen first. Konrad Lorenz, the ethologist, had geese following him everywhere when he was studying imprinting.

Tiglet was only a bit of fluff the size of a ping-pong ball when he set eyes on Kay McKeever, and he has been totally attached to her ever since. Tiglet barely tolerates the strange feathered creatures that hoot and call from the outdoor cages. He will never mate because he identifies with people, not owls. He has tried, many times, to court Kay.

Because of the imprinting, animals like Tiglet and Wheeper cannot return to the woods. They are totally dependent. The aim of the rehabilitation center is to return the birds to their natural habitat.

"My first year at school was the beginning of the owl business," said Kay. "I was six years old when my father told me the facts of life about who eats who. I had admired a family of wrens. But they were eaten by a hawk, and I was crushed."

Her father told her about animal predators and how they were doing what they had to do. He told her that as long as there had been a world of animals, there had been predators, and that man is the worst predator of all.

"I thought a lot about it," said Kay, "and from that time on I fought the good fight for the predators of the world. I made certain that the other kids at school knew that wolves and hawks and owls were very important. I dare say my family suffered through this stage with me. I was particularly taken with a small woolly grey toy owl, and nobody touched that owl but me. Owls were always special for some reason I cannot explain."

Although she was an ardent bird watcher with her father, she was not involved in anything even remotely connected with birds during school or after. She was bored by science courses and stayed away from them as much as possible. But she was fascinated by flight, and after she graduated from high school she studied navigation and learned to fly an airplane, logging many solo hours.

Years later, she and her husband, Larry, settled into a country house in the fruit orchards of the Niagara Peninsula, a region between Lake Erie and Lake Ontario. In 1965, while Jane Goodall was learning about chimpanzees in Africa, Kay McKeever began her long association with owls.

One day a friend called and asked, "Would you like to have a screech owl?"

"I knew nothing about them, but I said yes," Kay said.

After weeks of ardent care, the tiny owl died in convulsions. Kay was upset, but she had the good sense to have the bird autopsied. The report showed death from pesticides. She had been feeding it juicy worms from the fertile soil around the fruit trees. It had not occurred to anyone at the time that the insect spray lavished on the fruit trees had washed into the soil and then into the earthworms.

Kay was determined that such a thing would never happen again. Shortly afterward, she became the caretaker for three more owls. And she began to study everything she could find about these birds of prey.

Owls are crepuscular creatures, which means that they like to hunt during the twilight hours (when the mice are out looking for food). Although they can see better than we do in dim light, they see even better in daylight and not at all in total darkness. Their exceptionally large eyes gather maximum light, but they depend upon their keen hearing to help them find their prey. In one experiment, scientists put an owl in a totally dark room and then released a mouse among some dry leaves. The owl found the mouse instantly by following the noise the mouse made.

Some owls look as though they have ears, but they are really only tufts of feathers. An owl's ears are actually long slits under the feathers on either side of the head, extending the length of the skull in some kinds of owls. These slits are covered with loose feathers that lift when the owl is listening intently. The eardrums are larger than those of any other bird. But most of the sound is gathered by the facial disks—round, saucer-shaped disks on the face that give the owl its wide-eyed look.

The owl's beak works like strong tweezers and is used to tear food apart. But the owl does not kill with its beak. Instead, it uses its strong talons, which can grip like a vise and inflict deep wounds. Unlike those of a hawk, the owl's talons can go forward and in reverse. An owl keeps two toes forward and two back in order to hang onto a perch, but it can swing one toe forward for attack.

Owls look larger than they really are because they fluff their feathers to keep themselves warm in winter and cool in summer. A layer of soft down next to the owl's body, under the feathers, acts like insulated underwear. There is no whir of wings when an owl flies because the edges of the flight feathers are soft.

Much of what Kay learned about owls came from books, but most of it came from trial and error.

For example, Kay thought, as most people did, that owls needed to eat whole animals, including the fur and feathers, in order to clean their gullets when they threw up pellets.

Owl pellets are small, undigested ovals of fur and bones left over from birds or rodents that the owls have eaten. Owls throw them up. By examining owl pellets, you can find out exactly what an owl has eaten. That is how scientists know how many rats or mice an owl can eat.

Kay discovered, however, it wasn't the fur or feathers they needed at all, but the calcium in the bones of their prey. She found hard-shelled insects and ground them together with beef heart, liver and other organs the butcher would sell cheaply, and some calcium in the form of bone meal. "And then, using my limited art ability," Kay said, "I sculpted them into tiny naked mice. To tempt the owls, I added fur clipped from the grey hair of two Schnauzer dogs. It was a success. The owls ate and they stayed healthy."

As people heard of Kay's success with owls, they brought birds to her. Without intending to, she found herself becoming more and more involved. She needed cages and a source of food for the owls.

The McKeevers built all the cages, which blend into the wooded slopes around the house. They designed them, bought the lumber, and did all of the construction themselves. There are twenty-two outdoor flight cages ranging in size from 500 to 700 square feet. Although the McKeevers paid for the majority of the cages, some of them are now funded by conservation groups, foundations, and interested individuals. Twelve more are being built, in a variety of designs to accommodate different owls' needs. Some are W-shaped; others look like an E, which allows the birds to keep their territories separate and to sort out their own choices of mates. There are also eighteen indoor hospital cages.

What began as a hobby has become a full-time job, and much of it is hard, grubby work. Every day cages must be cleaned, rats defrosted, owls fed with freshly killed mice, mouse cages cleaned, mice fed, injured birds exercised, wounds dressed and treated. There are no days off when you care for animals.

Today, universities and hospital labs in Toronto and Hamilton, Ontario, keep the owls supplied with rats. Kay raises mice for the live feedings, and she gets baby chicks from a hatchery. Fifteen or more pounds of rats are used in one day's feeding. Kay uses a written schedule to keep track of who eats what and how much. The owls' diet rotates every seven days. There are four rat days, one mouse day, and two baby chick days. The change in diet supplies the owls with food most like the food they would eat in the wild.

Even without a calendar, Kay knows the first day of hunting season. On that day, injured owls begin to arrive at their hospital. Conservation officers, police, game wardens, and bird watchers bring in owls that have been shot. Ninety percent of the owls at the center are injured by guns. Others may have flown into a moving car at night when the lights confused them. Some have flown into television towers or picture windows. All the owls they help have been, in Kay's words, "interfered with"—that is, injured by humans.

Each new arrival is carefully examined in a room in Kay's basement that was originally a laundry room but was gradually converted to a hospital treatment room. There is a lighted wall box for reading X-rays and a special cage with a heat lamp to warm birds in shock.

First aid, warmth, and some food usually get an owl through the first shock of injury and capture. Birds requiring surgery are taken to a veterinarian, who can administer an anesthetic and treat them in a fully equipped operating room.

Through the years, Kay has experimented with many kinds of gadgets to help the birds recover. She uses a knit fabric to make a body sling, much like a sock, that slips over the owl's body to support and protect broken wings. She has made a sling from which the injured bird can be suspended comfortably with its feet just reaching a perch. It is important for an owl to learn to grip a branch after injury or it will never survive.

Early in her work with owls, Kay decided that her center would never become just a series of cages where crippled birds lived out useless lives. Even after she has made the birds comfortable, she tries to give them more. She feels that quality of life is the most important consideration.

She would like to return all the owls to the wild, of course. But some of them, in spite of care and intense treatment, can never fly well enough to defend themselves or hunt. If they cannot regain the use of their legs in order to perch, or cannot feed themselves, they are killed quickly and kindly with an injection. But even those birds' lives are not considered a waste. Each, in a way, contributes to science. Each is carefully examined, weighed, and measured so that information can be included in scientific notes. What is learned from those owls can help other owls.

The injured owls that recover enough to care for themselves in the protection of captivity but cannot care for themselves in the wild are also used. They become the breeding pairs. From one pair of barn owls, thirty healthy offspring were released from the center in two and a half years.

Owls are nature's rat traps. They fill an important niche in the food chain, and farmers depend upon them whether they know it or not. A farm without owls and hawks around it is going to have a big population of rats and mice to nibble on corn and grain.

Kay is doing what she can to see to it that these rat traps have a farm to hunt around.

Ever since the publication of *Born Free,* the book about lions, most people know that when man interferes with the life of a wild

Kay McKeever talks to Wheeper, a great horned owl who has been imprinted on Kay so that he can never be free. (K. Bruce Blanchard)

animal, that animal can no longer fend for itself in the wild. Just as the lions had to be taught to hunt by Joy Adamson, so the owls are taught to hunt by Kay McKeever. She calls it "hunting therapy," and it is her substitute for the teaching skills an owl usually learns from its parents.

The young birds born to the captive owls are always treated as wild birds. They are not named or tamed or handled, so they will not become dependent on humans.

Release training begins in early spring, when the birds are moved from their usual cages to special ones. The training cages are built with wide fiberglass panels around the bottom to make them mouse-proof—there are no holes through which a mouse can scoot. Until this time, the owls have been waited on like visitors in a plush hotel. Each day at the same time, freshly killed mice have appeared in the clean feeding boxes in their regular flight cages. Suddenly, no food arrives.

Now the mice are alive. They are put into the cage and left to scurry through the rustling dead leaves just as they would in the woods. But the mice are laboratory-born and raised, and they don't even know they are supposed to be afraid of these feathered monsters. So the mice run along the perches looking at the owls, and the owls are puzzled by these furry things that are sharing their quarters.

On the first day of this new feeding schedule, the owls act annoyed, sort of asking, "Where's the food?" On the second day, when they are really hungry, the owls begin to make a racket when Kay passes the cage on her way to feed the others. But still there is no food lying neat and dead in the food box. Only those running furry things. Finally, on the third or fourth day, the hunger seems to trigger some deep, unused instinct, and one of the owls pounces clumsily at a startled mouse. By the second pounce, the open talons making a quick, clean kill, every-thing seems to click into place, and the owl has become the hunter, the mouse trap nature intended it to be. The mice, too, suddenly be-come educated, and the word goes around among the mice to stay hidden. There is no more scrambling of mice across the perches.

After the owl has learned its part, the McKeevers have to find a place to release it. They drive around the countryside looking for likely territories. The best place for a barn owl is, of course, around a barn, preferably filled with animals, and corn fields or a corn crib where mice and rats raise their families. They look for a farm away from highways, and they like to find one with old buildings so the owls can fly in and out of cracks and broken boards. Kay once persuaded a farmer to cut holes in a brand-new barn just for the owls.

When they spot a likely-looking farm, Kay gets out of the car to imitate her barn owl call, a talent she has developed well. If she gets no answer, she can safely assume there are no owls using that territory.

When she releases an owl, she has a great sense of accomplishment. But she also feels a sadness. It is difficult not to feel an attachment for an animal you have raised.

When the McKeevers began their owl project, the neighbors probably thought they were crazy. Who else would buy meat at a butcher shop for owls? But stranger still, what kind of person would hire someone to build a nest?

The McKeevers had watched a pair of great horned owls courting in nearby trees. They had heard the calls and watched the male trying to seduce the female with no success.

"Good heavens," said Kay, "those poor young things don't have a nest."

Owls seldom build their own nests. They prefer to occupy an abandoned nest, sometimes a hawk's nest. Kay and Larry searched the area but could not find an empty nest.

"So I called the tree-pruning people," said Kay, "and explained that I wanted a nest built in a fifty-foot oak tree."

"You want a *what*, lady?" asked the man on the phone.

Two men arrived and listened while Kay described how to build an owl's nest. But they kept exchanging glances of disbelief.

Following directions, they built a platform fifty feet up the tree. They put drainage holes in the wooden bottom and attached small sides to keep nesting material from falling out. They hoisted bundles of sticks, twigs, and pine needles up the tree.

"How do you want 'em put in here, lady?" called the man in the tree.

Kay told him to put the large sticks down first, then smaller ones, until finally the top layer was soft pine needles.

"Now make a depression in the middle. You know, shape it like a nest."

"How do I do that?" hollered the man.

"Just sit in it and move your backside around a little, Harry," called the helper on the ground.

Although Kay speaks lightly of the owls and the things she has done with them, she takes the work seriously. She does not allow the public in to see the owls because visitors disturb the birds. It is not a zoo. But she does show groups of college students and other ornithologists around.

When Kay enters one of the owls' enclosures, she keeps her head bowed a little. "Don't look an owl in the eye," she tells you. "Direct eye contact is a threat."

Kay, however, can look directly at some of the long-time residents, like Tiglet and Wheeper and Grannie, who is a spectacled owl from South America. Kay rescued her from a horrible roadside zoo where she had been existing in a crate barely big enough for the owl to stand up in. She can talk to Holy Nellie, a beautiful snowy owl who had been shot and who cannot be released. His name came from Kay's comment each morning when she went into his cage and saw the mess he made. "Holy Nellie," she would exclaim.

The most recent triumph at the center, and cause for great rejoicing, was the birth of the first baby screech owls ever hatched in captivity by disabled wild parents. "And they are releasable," Kay wrote, underlining, "It's working, it's working!"

"Perhaps someday," Kay McKeever says with longing, "people will appreciate the owl. And this place won't be necessary."

Chapter Six

Hope Buyukmihci and the Keepers of the Stream

A scratchy noise from a corner of the living room was a signal for anyone nearby to lift the wooden trap door in the floor next to the couch. A pair of bright brown eyes peered with a nearsighted look from the opening, and a young beaver hoisted himself out of the hole. It was Chopper. Holding his small front paws close to his chest, he shook his chubby body and looked around the room. Then he began his daily tour of his indoor territory.

He tasted a wooden table leg and took a few chomps from the wooden door frame before someone stopped him. He plodded like a determined old man on his webbed hind feet, dragging his scaly tail and moving anything not fastened down. He shoved things under chairs like a kid cleaning his room.

One day he grabbed a paperback book with his great orange teeth and hurried back down his hole. Much later, the book was found in Chopper's indoor den in the basement, apparently being used as a pillow. If any of the human family forgot to put a book away, they were sure to find it, wet and chewed, in Chopper's quarters.

The "beaver in the house" time was one of the most exciting of Hope Buyukmihci's years with the beavers. Her name is pronounced *Bew-yuk-muk-chu.* It is a Turkish name, without an accent on any particular syllable.

The home Hope shares with the beavers is at Unexpected Wildlife Refuge, and it is truly unexpected as you approach on a sand road through the scrubby pines and greenbrier of southern New Jersey. It is two hundred acres of wild surrounded by farmland and highways, less than an hour's drive from Philadelphia.

Chopper was a two-week-old beaver kit whose family had been killed when a farmer dynamited their lodge near a Midwestern farm. For six weeks the baby stayed with a family who fed him cereal and pet formula from a bottle. They let him swim in the bathtub with the children and they rocked him to sleep at night. But the family loved the animal enough to know that a beaver is not a house pet, that it should be free.

The problem was finding a place where the beaver could not only be free but would not be trapped or hunted. They heard of Hope Buyukmihci's work with the beavers at her home which she named Unexpected Wildlife Refuge. So Chopper was sent to New Jersey.

Hope redecorated her living room for the young beaver's arrival. For twelve years she had hoped for a beaver in the house. Each spring when the new beaver kits emerged from a nearby lodge and allowed Hope to pet them, she was tempted to take one as a pet. But she knew that was wrong. She did not want to make an animal dependent on humans.

Now at last there was a chance to take a house beaver and teach it to be independent.

She put a wading pool, made from a six-foot metal cement mixing tub, in one corner of the room. Wall-to-wall plastic covered the tile floor and most of the furniture. And after the snatching of the paperback, Hope added a barricade to the bookshelves.

Chopper arrived in a carrying case. He stepped out of it looking like an unsure tourist just off the plane. He looked around and then began a cautious, waddling tour of his new home. It did not take him long to adopt both the room and the people as his own.

While Chopper was enjoying the living room, Hope and her husband, Cavit, had begun to dig a sixty-foot tunnel lined with tile from the edge of the cove, where the other beavers lived, to an opening in their cellar. A wooden ramp connected the tunnel to the hole in the living room floor.

"Meanwhile," said Hope, "we introduced Chopper to October, the wild mother beaver living in the cove."

Cavit took Chopper to the spot where they fed the beavers each evening and held the kitten on his lap. October appeared. She circled around the water several times before going to eat from their hands. Finally, October approached the little beaver.

Chopper leaned forward, his eyes wide. October floated nearby. She raised her muzzle and touched noses with the beaver kitten. For a long moment the old beaver examined the newcomer. Then, with a great sigh, she lowered herself and turned away.

"Her reaction had not been hostile," said Hope, "though it lacked somewhat in welcome." It didn't seem to bother Chopper, however, and he snuggled down on Cavit's lap to chew on an apple.

When the tunnel was finished, Chopper ignored it. Hope had to show him how to use it. She pushed Chopper down into the ramp and closed the door. Then she ran to the cove where she called, "Here Chopper, come Chopper."

That first trip took Chopper ten minutes. But once he learned to use the tunnel, he could zip through it in no time.

When he reached the cove that first time, he acted like a child at a picnic. He streaked underwater to one side of the small bay and popped up far from Hope. Then he dashed back to be petted. He rolled over and over in the water.

Chopper lived in and out of the house and cove for many months. Sometimes he used the pipeline tunnel; other times he walked overland from the lake. A trap door was put in the porch and a cowbell was hung from the kitchen door so that he could let the family know when he wanted to come in.

Gradually, Chopper began to use his freedom. "The first night he went by himself out of the cove and into the lake," said Cavit, "we felt like parents whose son has gone out on his first date. We could not sleep until he came home at 12:30 A.M."

After that Chopper went to the lake frequently. He found his way to a Girl Scout Camp a mile downstream—through a neighbor's land, across Unexpected Road, another half-mile downstream, across another road, up a dike, and finally into the lake.

The Girl Scouts loved him. He swam with them, nuzzling them underwater and allowing them to pet him. But one summer day a canoe appeared on the lake. Shortly after there was a terrible commotion. The man in the canoe was beating at the water with his paddle. When it was over, Chopper was dead.

The man in the canoe claimed the wild animal was trying to get into his boat to attack him. He did not know that beavers don't attack or that Chopper was tame. Hope and Cavit were crushed. They felt responsible for Chopper's death.

"If people knew animals, they wouldn't harm them," says Hope. "Misunderstanding, that's what it is."

Hope is doing what she can to correct that kind of misunderstanding. And she is not one to do things halfway. She uses no animal products. She does not wear leather, eat meat, or drink milk. She does not use cheese, eggs, butter, or honey. Her immediate goal is to stop all trapping of beavers, first in New Jersey and eventually everywhere.

She spends a great deal of time writing letters to politicians, urging them to vote for laws protecting beavers. She spends a lot of time visiting schools and telling children about beavers, who are the natural conservationists.

If she could live to see the day that all hunting and trapping of

Hope Sawyer Buyukmihci, feeds two of the wild beaver kits at Unexpected Wildlife Refuge in New Jersey. (Photo by The Beaver Defenders)

animals would be stopped, she would consider her life truly worth-while. Hope is wiry, hard-working, tough, and very gentle. It takes hard outdoor labor to watch over a wildlife refuge, patrolling its boundaries against poachers and hunters, clearing trails, and making sure there is cover and food for the birds and other animals.

As a young woman, Hope worked at Cornell University illustrating the original *Field Guide to Natural History*. At Cornell, she met a young man from Turkey who was studying metallurgy. She married him, and they lived in Turkey for five years.

There she discovered a life totally different from anything she had ever known. Where she had always been self-sufficient, she discovered that in Turkey women had no rights, made no decisions. That was difficult for Hope to bear, but even worse was watching the ways in which animals were treated. She horrified her husband's relatives one day by running out to try to rescue a small, overloaded donkey that had fallen to its knees and was being beaten to make it get up.

When the Buyukmihcis returned to America, Hope was deter-mined to raise their three children in a place where they could learn to love nature and watch animals. They bought a small, rundown cottage in the middle of what was to become the refuge. All of them worked to rebuild the house, but Hope spent more and more of her time walking through the woods or sitting at the pond.

Each day she reported to her family on the animals she had seen —the grouse, flying squirrels, foxes, bluebirds. And each day as she wandered near the old beaver lodge, she hoped to see the beavers.

Even though beavers are orderly animals, keeping regular hours, it is difficult to see them because they are active at twilight. Hope began to watch and wait at the same time every day. Her husband suggested that she put food out for them, to lure them to her. So she cut poplar and aspen branches and laid them near the dam. Every morning when she returned to the spot, the branches were gone. But there was no other sign of the beavers.

One night she decided to stay and watch. "But I have always been afraid of the dark," she said. "Now the question was, which was stronger, my fear of the dark or my desire to study beavers?"

She took a flashlight and blankets and went down the familiar path to the pond. "Heavy branches closed overhead, and the full moon was blotted out by clouds. I stumbled, and when the blankets caught and held on branches I felt trapped. The way ahead was like a wall, and the blackness followed behind like padded feet."

But she wrapped herself in the blankets and made herself stay in spite of the hooting of owls, crackling of branches, and scuffling noises in the night. Finally she fell asleep. She awakened the next morning to bright sunlight and a red squirrel scolding overhead. Then she inspected the dam. Fresh mud had been pushed up and sections of peeled poplar branches shoved into place. The beavers had been there while she slept.

After that, she spent many nights at the pond, and each morning the food was gone. Then winter set in, and she stopped sleeping at the pond's edge.

The following spring, as soon as there was nothing left of winter but a chill in the air, Hope returned to her watch. "Aren't you ever going to stay home with us?" her children began to ask. "All you ever talk about is beavers."

But spring moved into summer, and still she had seen no beavers. She thought of building a blind, a place to hide, but she wanted the beavers to accept her as she was. Then one evening, as the light was just disappearing and Hope sat reading at the dam, "I heard a small gurgle, and looking up, saw a broad black nose poke out from the water not six feet away. Up rose the head of a big beaver, her seal-like whiskers all coated with pollen scum from the surface of the water. She climbed the dam four feet from me, chose a stick of leafy poplar, and settled down to eat with only the end of her flat, rounded tail in the water. I named her Whiskers."

When Whiskers and the other beavers no longer smacked the water when they saw Hope, she knew they had accepted her presence. After that, Hope's acquaintance with the beavers grew quickly.

The beaver is an amazing animal. Fossil bones tell us that beavers grew to be eight feet tall in prehistoric times. Even now the beaver is the largest rodent in North America, weighing in at more than fifty pounds when fully grown.

The beaver's body works wonderfully well for his life style. His flat tail is covered by horny plates that look like scales. It is not used as a shovel or a trowel for carrying mud, but works as a rudder to help the beaver steer and dive. It is a mat to sit on while he grooms his fur, and a prop to lean against while he gnaws a tree. He uses it to smack the water so hard that it sounds like a gunshot when he wants to warn other beavers to stay hidden.

With enormous lungs and the ability to store oxygen in muscles and blood, the beaver can stay underwater for fifteen minutes. And he is just about waterproof because of valves that close off his ears and nose, and a transparent membrane that covers his eyes like a diver's goggles. A flap of fur closes behind his teeth so he can chew underwater and eat stored food under the ice in winter.

A beaver is a gentle, easygoing kind of animal. He poses no threat to any of his neighbors. One naturalist called the beaver pond a miniature sanctuary because it is a home for otters, muskrats, and water birds of all kinds, as well as turtles, fishes, and shore animals.

Although the beaver is armed with razor-sharp, chisellike teeth, he uses them on wood, not prey. Like other rodents, the beaver's teeth never stop growing, but they wear away against each other or against hard wood. If they did not, they would grow in a circle. Beaver skulls have been found in which the teeth had pinned the jaws together, starving their owners. The outer surface of the orange teeth is covered with hard enamel. The inner surface is not, so it wears more quickly than the outer, making the chisellike point.

The beaver's fur is like a wet suit in two layers. The long, coarse guard hairs on top keep the dense inner fur dry. A beaver grooms himself continually. He must keep the outer fur oiled and clean in order to stay warm in sub-zero temperatures. He grooms with his combs—the two split nails of his hind feet. He rubs a gland at the base of his tail that secretes an oil called castoreum. Then he combs the oil through the fur.

Hope has seen the beavers nip out matted bits of fur, just as a cat will do in grooming.

People who work all the time are called "eager beavers." Beavers have the reputation of working all the time, but they play a great deal, too. On long summer days, or in Indian summer after the lodge is winterized and food is stored, the beavers loaf, sleep, eat, and explore the canals they build off the main pool.

One day Hope put on her bathing suit, gritted her teeth, and stepped into the cold pond water where some beaver kits were playing. Gently she lowered herself into the dark, chilly water. The young beavers swam around her, nibbled her toes, dived under her and between her legs like wild children. She could not follow them to their lodge behind the dam, but she stayed as long as she could in the cove.

Long before men could read or write or build dams, beavers were the keepers of the streams, building ponds that kept the water levels high. And when the beavers had cleared the land around that pond, they moved downstream to build a new dam. The old pond gradually filled in with silt; eventually it became a swamp, then a rich, fertile meadow.

When a beaver moves into a new neighborhood, he digs a temporary burrow in a mud bank, with a doorway beneath the water and a tunnel slanting upward. Then he begins to build a dam and a lodge.

The beaver chops down trees with his sharp teeth. He turns his head sideways and bites out the wood. Then he must cut the big tree into manageable pieces to drag to the nearest water. Once the wood is in the water, the beaver can easily haul the wood to the dam, where he rams it into the mud. Other branches and debris wash downstream, catching in the crisscross of sticks until a good-sized barrier crosses the stream. The beavers carry mud and grass between their chests and front paws and pack it between the sticks to anchor them and firm up the dam. Sometimes they walk upright on the dam carrying their loads of mud. The lodge is built of mud and sticks, with the entrance beneath the water and a carpet of wood shavings to keep the floor dry.

In winter the beaver lodge ices over, making it an impenetrable fortress from fox, bobcat, or other predator that might be looking for beaver kits for dinner. One winter evening when Hope walked across the frozen pond for signs of beaver life, she heard the snap and growl of ice contracting and ripping. In the moonlight she could see air bubbles under the clear ice where beavers had released their breath as they gnawed underwater. She crouched on the bank, chilled but fascinated by the stillness. Then suddenly there was a sound so unexpected that she could not place it for a moment. It was a chorus of beavers, mewing and humming, first one tone and then another like a harmony, coming from inside the lodge.

"To this duet was added a third voice, then a fourth, vocal music at its best, a quartet humming in exquisite harmony . . . the joyous voices of young beavers, snug in their winter lodge."

And while she listened to the kits, she saw the silhouette of Greenbrier, the father, against the moonlight snow. He had broken through the ice, hauled himself onto the dam, and begun to gnaw.

"I realized he was grinding ice away to keep a channel open while water swirled black and swift around him, almost washing him off his feet," Hope reported.

She said it was a vivid contrast—this father animal working to protect his home while his young sang at their play.

The beaver's lush fur was the cause for his near extinction. Because this fur became popular, particularly for men's top hats, the beaver was trapped and hunted as though it would last forever. But the beaver became extinct in Europe, and in only a few years it was almost extinct in the new America as well. In 1700, so many beaver pelts were taken to Montreal for sale that the shippers burned three-quarters of them in order to keep them valuable. They could get higher prices with fewer pelts. By 1800, there were three hundred beavers, by rough count, in New York State. Then the trail to the Oregon Territory opened, primarily to hunt beavers. The only thing that saved the animal was a change in fashion. Someone invented a machine that made equally good felt from silk, and when the Prince of Wales began wearing a silk hat, no one wanted to be seen in a "beaver."

Gradually, the beaver has been allowed to repopulate in America and Canada. But now and again he runs into civilization, and where man and animal clash, man usually wins. A beaver dams a stream, the water floods a highway, the beavers have to go. Hope believes that beavers would restore the natural water levels if allowed to go unhampered, and we would no longer have droughts or water shortages.

Now that Hope's children are grown and have left home, she devotes most of her time to the Beaver Defenders, an organization she started. She writes a newsletter that goes not only to its members but to politicians as well. She fights on two fronts—one to teach people that beavers are nature's hydraulic engineers, and the other to teach people not to hunt.

She has discovered that people are fearful of nature preserves close to home for two reasons. They fear she is harboring animals that might raid the farmers' fields one day, or they assume she is "saving" the animals for her own family hunting. So she continues to patrol the borders of the preserve during hunting season, and she continues to visit schools to teach children the value of animals.

Hope believes that as long as hunting is big business, it will continue. Hunting licenses are the main source of income for conservation departments, and they, in turn, encourage hunting. She says, "The wildlife protection officers do little more than run a nationwide shooting gallery with living targets."

She does, of course, get many arguments. But she fights for what she believes in, and she believes that animals have the right to exist without man's interference.

One day, a boy in a school group she was visiting said, "Why not shoot animals? That's what they're there for."

Hope answered him with a quotation from a Greek poem that says, "Boys throw stones at frogs in jest, but the frogs die in earnest."

Hope Buyukmihci's beavers continue to live. The Beaver Defenders continue to grow.

Chapter Seven

Karen Pryor and the Creative Porpoise

The porpoise shows at the Ocean Science Theater at Sea Life Park in Makapuu Point, Waimanalo, Hawaii, had been going smoothly for some time—so smoothly that Karen Pryor, the curator of mammals at the park, decided that they were not exciting any more. So she and one of the trainers thought it might be fun to show the audiences the first steps in training a porpoise by reinforcing, or rewarding, the animal with a piece of fish when it performed correctly. They wanted to show how trainers waited for the animal to do something spontaneously and then let the animal know they wanted it to do it again. That is called conditioning.

The first time it was easy. Malia, the small porpoise, was swimming around the tank, waiting for a cue or signal that would tell her what she was supposed to do. But the trainer did nothing. There was no cue. The porpoise became impatient after a minute or two and slapped her tail on the water, which is porpoise language for annoyance. The trainer immediately blew her whistle and tossed Malia a piece of fish.

Karen said, "That was enough for Malia. She got the message and slapped, ate her fish, slapped, ate, slapped repeatedly. In less than three minutes she was motorboating around the tank pounding her tail on the water, and the audience burst into applause."

That was exactly what they wanted to show the audience—the animal as a real being and not just a robot doing what it is told.

But when it was time for the next show and they wanted to show the next audience something new, they couldn't very well reward Malia for slapping her tail on the water. They had to wait for her to do something new. Malia grew more and more angry. Finally she threw her whole body into the air and came down sidewise, slapping the water with a huge splat. The trainer blew the whistle right away and threw Malia a fish. And Malia immediately began doing it over and over, pleased to have discovered what the trainer wanted and pleased to have her fish.

The trainers continued this routine for a couple of days, waiting at each performance for the animal to do something different so they could reward her and explain to the audience what had happened. Of course, there is more to training than waiting for an animal to do something, but in this case they wanted to show the first steps in training, those moments when the animal and the trainer are thinking together.

This procedure became more and more difficult, however, and there were one or two embarrassing shows when Malia went splashing around the tank doing all the things she knew, but nothing new that the trainers could reinforce and reward.

Then Malia solved the problem. "On the last show of the third day we let her out of the holding tank, and she swam around waiting for a cue. When she got no cues, instead of launching herself into a series of repetitions of old behavior, she suddenly got up a good head of steam, rolled over on her back, stuck her tail in the air, and coasted about fifteen feet with her tail out: "Look, Ma, no hands!"

After that, Malia seemed to be delighted with herself. She continued, show after show, to produce new and astonishing things to do. She spun in the air, swam upside down, revolved like a corkscrew.

"She thought of things we never could have imagined," said Karen.

The porpoise had obviously learned that the trainer was only rewarding things that had never been rewarded before. She was deliberately coming up with something new. "Sometimes she was very excited when she saw us in the mornings. . . . I had the unscientific feeling that she sat in her holding tank all night thinking up stuff and rushed into the first show with an air of "Wait till you see *this* one."

The animal had shown an example of first-order learning. Karen said, "Originality. Rare, but real, in animals. Almost never observable in a laboratory situation."

After the thrill of seeing Malia improvise, the trainers worked on another animal, and finally they began the long, exacting task of proving scientifically that the animals involved in the sessions were really creating, really "thinking."

Karen never meant to be a porpoise trainer, but she could hardly avoid the swimming pool in her yard, full of porpoises fresh from the ocean. These beautiful marine mammals were wild but friendly, as porpoises usually are, and they had already stumped the first team of trainers who tried to get them ready for the opening of Sea Life Park.

It really all began when Karen's husband, Tap, was a graduate student studying sharks. He needed a place to do his research—a place that would help support the research and allow him to be near his wife and three children. So he built a combination oceanarium-research station where he could learn and where people would pay to be entertained.

Things were going fairly well until three months before the scheduled opening, when everyone had just about given up trying to train the porpoises. The animals were intelligent and healthy, but the trainers were new at the job. "In fact," said Karen, "the porpoises had trained the trainers to give them fish for nothing."

When her husband suggested that she herself give it a try, Karen thought she might be able to handle it. She had trained a pony and a dog, and she kept thinking how nice it would be to have an easy job just four hours a day right near home.

"I had no idea I was about to be caught up in one of the major efforts of my life."

Being curator of mammals at Sea Life Park included scrubbing and hosing tanks, cutting up fish, and training trainers as well as animals.

Karen had majored in English literature at Cornell University, but she had done graduate work in biology at the University of Hawaii. She was not entirely new to the science of animals.

The porpoises, however, were new both to Karen and to the life they were going to lead. At Sea Life Park, the animals were called porpoises, although in many places the same species are called dolphins. They are small whales, and they all belong to a group of mammals called cetaceans. They breathe air, their young are born alive, and the babies are nursed for eighteen months to two years. The porpoise, or dolphin, breathes through a blowhole on top of its head and it emits a series of whistles, clicks, and rusty-hinge noises through this hole, too. Porpoises have no vocal cords, but they can also send out a series of signals from air pockets in the nasal passages. These sounds work like a sonar system. (Sonar is an abbreviation for *so*und *na*vigation *r*anging.) Man uses sound waves bounced from equipment in a submarine, for example, to let him know what is around. He got the idea from bats and porpoises. Underwater, where the sea is dark, the cetaceans can send out a series of sounds, sometimes at frequencies too high for humans to hear, and these sounds bounce back from objects they hit, like an echo. A porpoise can tell the difference between two similar fish by this system, even if it is blindfolded.

The porpoise's skin is smooth and firm. It feels like a peeled hard-boiled egg. A porpoise can live out of water, but its skin must be kept wet to keep it from cracking and to keep the animal from overheating through its thick layer of blubber.

Before Flipper, the TV porpoise, became popular and before aquariums began to exhibit these marine mammals, many porpoises were killed for shark bait as they gracefully leaped and played in the bays off the Florida and California coasts. But today more arguments are raging among scientists over the porpoise than almost any other animal. Some say that a porpoise is no smarter than a dog; others say the porpoise's brain—a brain more complex than man's—is capable of language.

Karen stands somewhere in the middle, admiring the porpoise for what it is—a beautiful marine mammal living in an entirely different kind of world from ours. She is a scientist-trainer, and she approached her new job with a combination of scientific doubt and practical ideas.

Another biologist, Victor Scheffer, suggested that instead of wondering whether porpoises can reason or plan ahead as humans do, we "should simply admire their complex brains . . . those mysterious organs which allow them to cope with a dim, cold, watery world in which we ourselves could not long survive."

It is not easy to watch porpoises in the wild. You can live near chimpanzees or beavers and watch caribou or wild horses with binoculars. But the porpoises dive deep where man cannot easily follow. A boat disturbs the daily routine of play and feeding, and a swimmer can't keep up with them. Radio tracking devices and markers can be put on porpoises if you catch them and release them, but that only tells where they go. So although not much is really known about the behavior of a group of these animals in the open ocean, a great deal can be learned about them as individuals in captivity.

Karen considered this, too. She said, "One cannot help but ask oneself if it is justified, this taking of animals from their home in the wild sea and subjecting them to the risks of captivity for the sake of scientific curiosity and public amusement. I think it is or I would not have been involved. So terribly little is known about cetaceans."

One of the first things Karen had to do was teach herself to be a trainer. She read what she could find, but there was very little available on the subject in 1963. Taming is one thing; training is another. There are some basic scientific rules for training. Karen had ninety days before the opening of the show in which to train the animals, and she said, "About nine-tenths of what I now know about training I would learn in the next three months."

First, the animal has to be conditioned. There are different kinds of conditioning. Pavlov was a Russian scientist who showed that animals and people can be conditioned by an unconscious process. He rang a bell when he fed his dogs, and eventually the dogs' mouths would water whenever they heard the bell, even if no food appeared.

Operant conditioning, which is used to train the porpoises, is a different process. In this kind of training, the animal makes something happen. He starts it; he is the operator. When he does some-

Karen Pryor and her daughter, Gale, then aged five, playing with Akamai, which means "smart one" in Hawaiian. It is one of the spinners trained to perform in the Sea Life Park programs. (*Sea Life Park*)

thing, a reward appears. It is the same sort of training you use when you ask your dog to sit up and speak and reward him with a snack.

Karen says, "Animals seem to enjoy this. I think they like to be able to make things happen for themselves."

A scientist, B. F. Skinner, discovered the principles of this operant conditioning, and it is often called Skinnerian conditioning.

The first thing that must be done is to teach the animals a signal that means that food or another reward is coming. You have to have some way to let the animal know what he is doing right. Karen decided on a whistle because the porpoises could hear it above or below the water and would not confuse it with other sounds. And it was a sound the trainer could make much more quickly than the pressing of a buzzer, for example. It didn't take long to whistle-condition the porpoises.

When Karen took over the training, there were several different kinds of porpoises to work with. There were spinners, which are about half the size of Flipper, who was an Atlantic bottlenose dolphin. There were two Pacific bottlenose porpoises, very much like Flipper, and there were two others closely related to the spinners except that they were spotted; their scientific name is *Stenella attenuata,* but they are called kikos, which is a Hawaiian word for "spots."

Karen started with the kikos, which were considered the "untrainables" because they were nervous and hadn't made any progress. The others had already learned about whistles and were doing some things asked of them.

Once an animal "understood" what the whistle meant, that sound could be used to change what he was doing a little at a time. That is called shaping. By blowing the whistle every time the animal turns to its right, for example, you can have the animal swimming in a tight circle to its right in just a few minutes. And with a little patience, and by using the whistle exactly at the right moment, you can have an animal do things it might never have done otherwise—like standing on its head and waving its tail in the air.

Every animal trainer has secret "recipes" for shaping the animals to do different things. Karen says there are probably as many ways to shape a single behavior as there are trainers to do it. It takes imagination and hard work.

"Shaping is fun," Karen wrote. "It is, however, only half of the training procedure. The other half is the establishment of cues or signals that let the animal know what you want and when you want it. Psychologists call this "bringing the animal under stimulus control." "It is a tricky business. When you have good stimulus control, you have, in effect, a sort of language between yourself and the animal and not entirely a one-way language. Your actions and his reactions begin to add up to mutual communication."

Karen found it exciting when an animal caught on to an idea. Sometimes, when an animal is on the wrong track, or is refusing to do what you ask, or is doing something that might be dangerous—like playing with a toy he could swallow—there has to be a punishment. You can't very well spank a porpoise. So the punishment becomes a "time out." The trainer picks up the pail of fish and just walks away. No fish, no reward. In all porpoise shows, the animals are trained to retrieve things that might be tossed or dropped into the pool, such as cameras, toys, and money, and part of the training is this "time out." If the porpoise does not bring the camera or coin to the trainer in return for a fish, the trainer calls a time out. It doesn't take long for the animal to learn what it must do to keep the fish coming.

Sometimes teaching a new behavior is a matter of waiting for the porpoise to do something you can reward and shape. You can't very well show a porpoise how to do a tail walk or a leap in the air. But when he does it on his own, you can blow the whistle and throw him a fish to tell him that you liked it. But, said Karen, "It meant walking around all day with your whistle in your teeth and a fish in your pocket."

Then the new behavior can be broken down into small steps so that the animal is shaped very gradually, one step at a time. Horse trainers, football coaches, and symphony conductors use this shaping, which Karen believes is a mixture of science and art.

Hiring trainers was part of Karen's job, too. She needed people who were used to being with large animals, who would not be afraid of a mouthful of large teeth snapping at them. Many of the trainers she hired had worked with horses, and many of them were women. Writing about the trainers, Karen said, "I, on the whole, prefer women as trainers. Men, in general, seemed to have a drawback: their egos. A man tended to feel that when the animal didn't respond correctly it was defying him. If women, in general, had a drawback as trainers, it was their kind hearts. The girls were willing, sometimes too willing, to let an animal get away with sloppy work, to let it slide rather than making it toe the line."

When the shows were going smoothly at Sea Life Park, and other trainers were handling most of the problems, Karen turned to other things when she had the time. The Navy was interested in how fast porpoises could swim. By their calculations, it was estimated that a porpoise ought to be able to do about twenty miles per hour. But there were so many reports of porpoises keeping up with huge destroyers and other ships that the Navy wondered if their calculations could be correct.

Karen whistle-conditioned a male teen-age bottlenose porpoise named Keiki. The plan was to take the animal into the open ocean for tests. "At that time nobody had ever taken a tame porpoise deliberately out to sea, with the idea of getting it back," she said.

Keiki enjoyed it. He liked chasing the boat, the way some dogs love chasing cars. But when all the test results were in, the Navy calculations were right. The porpoise swims at a top speed of twenty miles per hour. It can stay with fast ships by riding the wake, like a surfer rides a wave—in fact, it seems to be a worldwide porpoise sport, even older than the invention of boats. Humpback whales, speeding along the surface, have been seen with porpoises playing in their bow wake, hitching a ride.

Several porpoises trained at Sea Life Park took part in Navy research projects, some finding lost airplane parts on the ocean bottom, others carrying tools and messages to divers. Kai was a porpoise trained to wear a harness for tests to determine the depth a porpoise could dive. He had to dive through a hoop that broke a light beam to signal the depth and then return for his fish. He had done many days of dives, but the Navy needed just one more day of tests. Karen took off his harness that last day and put a soft nylon collar around his neck.

Kai worked hard. When he came up from a dive, he circled next to the boat, breathing repeatedly, resting before he obeyed the signal that told him to return to his cage to wait for the next dive. That day he suddenly circled around the boat, looked at the hoop and cage and Karen and the others in the boat. Then he took off. They watched as he leaped and chased the flying fish ahead of him, a wild animal that had suddenly chosen to go back to the wild. "Kai had earned his freedom," Karen wrote.

When the Navy ended that series of experiments, Karen reported that they didn't get the results they set out to find. But, as so often happens in science, they got some answers they didn't expect—and some questions for future work.

Karen Pryor is no longer working with the porpoises of Sea Life Park. She has taken on a bigger challenge. As a research scientist aboard the *David Starr Jordan,* she did a behavioral study of porpoises caught in tuna nets off the coast of Central America. She is now a consultant to the Porpoise Rescue Foundation, working on a solution to the problem of these animals and the tuna industry.

Konrad Lorenz, the scientist who is most often called the father of ethology, visited Karen at Sea Life Park. He said of her, "She is one of those who derive an inexplicable primal joy from just watching animals." And he added, "She is a born ethologist. She used conventional training techniques as a means of communication."

Chapter Eight

Eugenie Clark and
the Sleeping Sharks

Sunlight sparkled on bright blue-green water as a small boat dropped anchor. Three divers wearing black wet suits adjusted their scuba gear. One diver leaned over the side of the boat and peered into the water. It was so clear he could see the rainbow assortment of fishes swimming around the coral reef.

"Sharks below," he called.

"No problem," a second diver answered calmly. "Use this," she said, handing cans of shark repellent to the others.

When they had sprayed themselves all over with the repellent, the divers put on their masks and flipped backward out of the boat into the warm water. Two tiger sharks began to circle the divers. Silently they picked up speed to attack, but as they closed in on the swimmers, they slammed on invisible brakes. Suddenly their mouths seemed to be frozen open. They shook their heads as though trying to get rid of something. And the divers went about exploring the coral reef, unconcerned about the sharks.

So far, that scene is only make-believe. There is no shark repellent that really keeps sharks away, but there may be soon because Dr. Eugenie Clark was curious about a little fish called the Moses sole.

In 1960, Eugenie was netting fish in the Red Sea when she came across the fish known scientifically as *Pardachirus*; local fishermen called it the Moses sole. When she touched the fish, a milky substance oozed from the pores along its fins. It was slippery, and her fingers felt tingly and tight, the way they might feel if they fell asleep.

The Moses sole is a flatfish, like the flounder you buy at the market, and it got its name from a traditional story told in Israel. According to the legend, when Moses parted the Red Sea, this little fish was caught in the middle and split in half. Each half became a sole.

Eugenie is an ichthyologist, a scientist who studies fish. She was working at the Marine Laboratory at the Hebrew University in Elat, Israel, when she decided to find out more about the sole's poison. A scientist had reported the poisonous substance in 1871, but no one had studied it further. When Eugenie tested it on sea urchins, starfish, and reef fishes, she found that small doses killed these creatures quickly. She began to wonder how it would work on larger fishes, especially sharks.

Three reef whitetip sharks lived in a tank at the laboratory, and they ate anything dropped into the water. One day as Eugenie was experimenting with the fish, she found one small Moses sole that had not been completely "milked" of its poison. She put a string through its gills, which did not hurt it, and lowered the fish into the shark's tank. The moment the sole touched the water, the sharks swept toward it with mouths open wide. But when they got within a few feet of the fish on the string, the sharks' jaws seemed to be frozen open. They dashed away, shaking their heads as though trying to get rid of something awful. For six hours Eugenie watched the sharks approach the sole, and the reactions were the same each time the sharks swam near the poisonous fish.

The use of this poison as a shark repellent was an exciting idea. So far everything invented to keep sharks away has not worked on all sharks all the time. Streams of air bubbles used as a barrier along beaches eventually attracted sharks, who seemed to enjoy the feeling of the bubbles as they swam through them. Different dyes that swimmers can release in the water only hide the swimmer from the shark temporarily but cannot keep a really hungry shark away. Lifeboats on ships and Navy planes are sometimes equipped with plastic bags large enough to hold a person. Stranded in the water, the person inflates the top ring and crawls into the tubelike bag. A shark cannot follow the scent of a human inside this bag, nor can it see kicking legs or blood from a wound. But such bags are not carried as regular equipment by swimmers at an ocean beach. A substance that can be sprayed on, the way mosquito repellent is, would be perfect.

But before Eugenie could experiment further on the Moses sole, she had to leave the Elat laboratory, and other work claimed her attention for many years. It wasn't until 1974 that she was able to collect some of the fish and test the shark-stopping poison. After dozens of experiments in tanks and in the sea, a final test was arranged to find out how free-swimming sharks reacted to the live Moses sole.

An eighty-foot shark line, with ten shorter lines dropping from it, was stretched close to the rocky Israeli coastline three feet underwater at a point where a ledge dropped off to a depth of one thousand feet. Each of the ten dropper lines was baited with parrot fish, groupers, nonpoisonous flatfish, and the Moses sole. As Eugenie, her fourteen-year-old son, and other assistants snorkled quietly along the underwater ledge and watched the sharks approach the bait at dawn or sunset, they saw the poison at work.

One by one the fish were gulped down by hungry sharks, but the Moses sole remained untouched. When Eugenie wiped the skin of a Moses sole with alcohol to remove the poison and tossed the fish into the water, a shark would instantly eat it. It was an exciting discovery—a substance that could really stop a shark. Further work is being done now to make a chemical compound like the poison of the

Moses sole that can be used as a reliable commercial shark repellent.

Eugenie knew she wanted to be an ichthyologist long before she knew the word meant "someone who studies fish." Her father died when she was very small, and she lived in New York City with her mother. When her mother had to work on Saturdays, Eugenie went to the old aquarium in Battery Park at the tip of Manhattan. The hours went quickly for her as she watched the colorful reef fishes and the graceful sea turtles. It wasn't long before she had her own collection of guppies and swordtail platys, and she became the youngest member of the Queens County Aquarium Society. She learned to keep careful records of her fish and their scientific names.

All during elementary school and high school, her mother encouraged her in her new interest. When she went to Hunter College in New York for a degree in biology, Mrs. Clark, aware of the limited job possibilities for women, suggested that Eugenie add typing and shorthand to her studies. But Eugenie never had the time or interest to do it. When she graduated from Hunter College during World War II, there were not many jobs for biologists, so she worked for a while at the Celanese Corporation as a chemist and attended graduate school at night.

She wrote later on, "In the field of science, a Ph.D. degree is handy to have although not absolutely necessary. One of the most brilliant and accomplished ichthyologists in the country never went to college, although later he became a university professor. But a person without a formal education has a more difficult time proving his worth, especially when applying for a position. A Ph.D. among your qualifications helps start things out on the right foot. I hoped to get this degree . . . my career had enough other disadvantages for a woman."

In 1947, the U.S. Fish and Wildlife Service was planning a survey of the Philippine Island area for possible fisheries. They needed a person who knew fish and chemistry. Eugenie was qualified. She applied for the job and got it.

"Several people were surprised that a girl had been hired for the job. Then it was called to someone's attention in Washington that I was the only female scientist on the program. Some commotion followed. I got as far as Hawaii, but my passport was mysteriously delayed because, they told me, the FBI had to check my Oriental [Eugenie's mother is Japanese] origin and connections. As far as I know they are still checking. They never did tell me I was cleared. After weeks of waiting, I accepted my fate and handed in my resignation to waiting hands. They hired a man in my place."

Being stranded in Hawaii was no hardship for Eugenie. For an ichthyologist, the freedom to dive among the fascinating fishes around the Hawaiian volcanic reefs was as satisfying as being a cat free to roll in a meadow of catnip. But even that ended. She said later, "The longer you put off graduate studies, the harder it is to find the time and enthusiasm to go back to school." So she went back.

It take years of study and research to complete a Ph.D. Very often the original research requires going into the field to learn about the subject first-hand.

"Women scientists have to buck some difficulties when it comes to field work," said Eugenie, "but I had one decided advantage. A man in my position often has a family to support and is not free to travel. I was independent and free to go anywhere and do anything I liked, and there was only my own neck to risk."

Eugenie went many places. She learned to dive while studying at Scripps Institute of Oceanography in California. She used her diving skills constantly in Micronesia in the Pacific Ocean, where she collected the *plectognaths* she was studying. These are small fish that live mostly in tropical waters near coral reefs. They include the triggerfish, porcupine fish, puffer, filefish, and boxfish.

One of her research fellowships took her to the Red Sea, where she found the Moses sole and collected the elusive garden eels that burrow in the ocean bottom. They are long, smooth fish that sway gently with the water currents as they feed upon small ocean creatures.

In Cairo, Egypt, Eugenie married a doctor she had met during her studies in the United States. When they returned to the states, Eugenie began the less glamorous part of being a scientist—sorting through notes and writing the scientific results of things she had found. And she began to raise a family.

In 1955, she was delighted to be asked to start a marine laboratory in Florida. Her husband was ready to open a medical office, and he agreed that Florida would be a good place to live. With their first two children, they moved to Florida's west coast, and Eugenie became the director of the Cape Haze Marine Laboratory. At first the laboratory was only a small wooden building, twelve by twenty

Dr. Eugenie Clark working in her favorite laboratory . . . the sea. (Tsuneo Nakamura, Tokyo, Japan)

feet, built on skids so it could be moved if the first site did not work out. There was a dock and a boat for collecting. Eugenie decided her first job should be to collect and identify all the local fishes.

The day after she arrived, she received a phone call from a doctor who needed shark livers for cancer research. She checked with the man who was going to handle the boat, and even before supplies were unpacked, they were in the shark-hunting business.

There are about 250 different sharks in the world, ranging in size from the 24-inch dogfish studied in biology classes to the 60-foot giant whale shark that eats plankton and is so gentle that divers have hung onto its fins for a short ride. In between are the man-eaters we hear horror stories about. All the sharks belong to a group of fishes called cartilaginous. They have skeletons made not of bone but of cartilage, that bendable tissue our ears and noses are made of. And all the sharks are torpedo-shaped predators. They have many sets of razor-sharp teeth that they can fold back into a nonbiting position or thrust forward, ready to slice easily into prey. When a tooth is lost, another moves into place quite quickly.

The shark's always-staring eyes give it an evil appearance. It cannot blink or close its eyes for sleep, but it has a membrane that can cover the eye for protection.

Eugenie and her assistant began collecting some of the eighteen species of sharks found off the west coast of Florida. As she dissected hammerhead, nurse, lemon, and sand sharks on the dock, her children, neighbors, and children of visiting scientists watched. Sometimes she gave them jobs to do—measuring parts of the intestines, washing out a shark stomach, or hosing the dock after the dissection. Some of the sharks brought in on lines survived, and Eugenie wanted to know as much about the live animals as she knew about the organs she was weighing and measuring.

A stockaded pen, forty by seventy feet, was built next to the dock to hold the live sharks. A tiger shark, named Hazel, and a reddish color nurse shark, named Rosy, were two of the first guests in the pen, and a new problem arose. Nosy visitors, ignoring signs and fences, poked around and teased the animals. Eugenie was worried that both people and sharks would be hurt. When several of the sharks were killed by trespassers, Eugenie began to talk to groups in the community, especially at schools. She explained what sharks eat and how they live. Whenever people know about an animal, they fear it less. Soon the newspapers labeled her the "shark lady." It is a name that has stayed with her in spite of all her research with other sea creatures.

It wasn't long before Eugenie was involved in finding out how sharks learn. She enjoyed working with the live sharks day after day and getting to know the individual personalities of the animals.

When she set up experiments in which sharks would have to hit a target to receive the reward of food, one scientist warned her, "Don't be discouraged. It may take months." But he was wrong. The sharks learned quickly. When two lemon sharks learned that they could press an empty target and get food for it, Eugenie thought up harder problems for them to solve.

She trained them to swim to the end of the seventy-foot pen to pick up food after they pressed the target; and the female shark, who usually hung back and waited for the male to go first, quickly learned that if she circled the food drop area, she could pick up the male's reward while he was still at the target.

Eugenie stopped the tests during the winter months when the sharks lost interest in food, but she found that the sharks remembered everything they had learned when spring training began. She moved on to more complicated learning. She used targets of different sizes, shapes, and designs, and she found that sharks of the same species, like other animals, have great individual differences. Some are smarter than others.

Scientists from all over the world visited the Cape Haze laboratory, studying everything from parasites on sharks to microscopic life on algae. By the time Eugenie had been the laboratory's director for ten years, she had four children who enjoyed diving and helping her underwater explorations.

When Eugenie heard that there were "sleeping" sharks a diver could swim right up to, she was determined to find out more about them. With her daughter, Aya, and some research assistants, she went to Mexico's beautiful Isla Mujeres off the tip of the Yucatán Peninsula. There, in the warm, clear underwater caves, she found the great, sleek sharks of the requiem family—the notorious man-eaters. They were lying on the floor of the caves, looking half-asleep even though their open, staring eyes watched the divers swim toward them.

Ordinarily, these sharks must keep moving. They swim constantly in order to keep the oxygen-rich water flowing through their mouths and out over the gills. When they rest on the bottom, they must pump water over the gills, and that takes more energy than leisurely swimming. But in the caves the sharks were motionless. Even with divers churning up water and sand, and even with the glare of photographers' lights, the sharks acted as though they were tranquilized.

Eugenie and her team measured the depth and temperature of the water in the cave. They mapped the water currents by dropping dyes in the water and following their paths. They took water and rock samples for chemical analysis. And they noticed how clean the sharks looked compared to those caught by local fishermen. These cave sharks were not infested with the parasites found on most sharks.

They watched the "shark's faithful housekeeper," the small remora fish, as it worked around the eyes and mouths and into the gill slits of the resting sharks. The remora is a fish whose dorsal fin has evolved into a kind of suction disk on the top of its head. It can hitch a ride on a shark, sea turtle, whale, or even a ship by means of this suction disk. The remora picks up pieces of food dropped by its host. In the caves, however, these remoras worked diligently. Could it be that these "sleeping" sharks gathered in the caves for a health treatment? Were the caves cleaning stations?"

Eugenie discovered fresh water seeping into the caves, diluting the sea water. There was less salt in the caves than in the open ocean. She remembered that when she was a kid she would put her saltwater fish into fresh water for a little while so that the parasites would drop off. Perhaps the same thing was happening with the sharks. Maybe these eighteen-foot tiger and reef sharks were intelligent enough to seek comfort in the caves.

Eugenie had taught sharks to ring a bell and push targets for meals and to distinguish right from wrong targets at the Florida laboratory.

"Surely," she said, "they are capable of learning that in water of below-normal salinity, a condition they apparently must sense, annoying parasites loosen their grip."

The sharks may not know the water is less salty, but they know it feels good, so they go there. There are three such caves known around Mexico. Recently, some underwater caves full of sharks were reported around Japan. So many divers swarmed into the caves, catching sharks by the hundreds for food, that by the time Eugenie got to Japan to see them, the sharks had learned it was not safe to go to that cleaning station. Another cave was discovered near Japan, but Eugenie and other scientists are keeping its location secret to protect the sharks.

When asked about her life as a scientist, Eugenie said, "Being a scientist and a woman has some advantages, some disadvantages. It balances out. It takes some time to prove yourself initially, but then you get more credit than a man when you do accomplish something. For example, I am a diver, and when I dive into a cave with sharks it seems to be much more amazing than when a man does it."

The "shark lady" publicity has followed Eugenie, and no matter what she does, people think of her as the spear-carrying shark hunter. But she said, "I get just as excited about the garden eels in the Red Sea. Perhaps the discovery that thrilled me the most was the first hermaphroditic vertebrate, a fish that changes sex."

Looking for an excuse to go swimming one hot July day, Eugenie decided to take a census of the fish around a certain coral reef near the Cape Haze laboratory. She watched a tiny grouper fish, called *Serranus*. There were dozens of females swollen with eggs that would have to be laid and fertilized. But she could not find any males. No matter how long she followed some of these fish or what time of day she watched, no males appeared.

For a year she found no answers. But after many dives and long hours in the lab looking at fish under the microscope and watching live fish in lab tanks, she finally solved the mystery. *Serranus* is an hermaphrodite—an animal with both male and female parts. There are a few vertebrates that start life as one sex and turn into another, functioning as both in a lifetime, but never at the same time. *Ser-*

ranus turned out to be the first vertebrate found in which every individual could function at the same time as a male and female, able to fertilize itself. It seems, however, that this self-fertilization is used only in an emergency when a mate is not available. It was an exciting discovery that will probably lead to other investigations.

Eugenie Clark obviously loves what she does. "If from my research mankind gains some practical application or benefit, this is added delight and satisfaction to my work," she said. "But this is not what drives me to study late into the night or to watch a fish on the bottom making some strange maneuver until all the air in my scuba tank is gone and I hold my breath for those last few seconds."

Chapter Nine

Dian Fossey and
the Gentle Giants

Five enormous black male gorillas, their roars echoing through the silent forest, charged toward the tall woman who had been watching from a clump of thick vegetation. She knew if she ran they would only pursue her, so she turned to face them. When the leader was only three feet from her, she spread her arms like a street-crossing guard and shouted at the top of her voice, "Whoa!"

All five gorillas stopped in their tracks. They looked at her and at each other, a quizzical expression in their eyes, then turned and ambled away to join the rest of their group feeding nearby.

Dian Fossey took that risk because she knew the gorillas. She had been living in the Virunga Mountains, in Zaire, not far from the equator in Africa, and like Jane Goodall, she had been studying a vanishing group of primates.

Dian was an occupational therapist working with children in a hospital in Louisville, Kentucky, when she read about a man who had studied gorillas in Africa for a year. Dr. George Schaller had made some important observations, and he had amazed many "great white hunter" type of explorers by following gorillas without a gun.

Far from being the "monster" of King Kong fame, the gorilla was found to be a peaceful, unhurried creature, living in small groups, feeding only on vegetation, fearing nothing but man.

Dian had always loved animals, and she had studied veterinary medicine for a while before she became a therapist. When she read about the gorillas, she was determined to see for herself. She borrowed money and went to Africa for two months. Part of the trip took her to the Virunga volcanoes, where she met a couple who were photographing gorillas. It was there that she saw the gorilla's giant footprint, an impression in the wet mud that dwarfed the mark of man. She heard the terrifying shriek of a gorilla through the stillness for the first time. And she loved it all.

Back in Louisville, she wrote an article about her safari for the local newspaper, describing her impressions of Africa and telling of the need to protect the great gorillas.

One day Dr. Louis Leakey showed up at the hospital where Dian worked and asked her to go to Africa. Just like that. She was astounded. The great scientist was in America on a lecture tour, and he had seen her newspaper article.

When she protested that she was too old (she was thirty-seven at the time), he told her that was nonsense—she was mature and quite capable of filling this job. Two other women had attempted the gorilla study, but for one reason or another they could not habituate these beautiful primates.

Dian had no training for this work, but Dr. Leakey assured her, as he had assured Jane Goodall, that he wanted untrained people. "I want open minds. I don't want preconceived opinions. I just want people to go out there and use their eyes and look," he told her.

Speaking at a meeting years later, Dian described how Dr. Leakey had tested her occasionally. Once, in front of the museum in Nairobi, he asked, "What do you see there?"

Looking carefully, Dian told him she saw a spider web, thinking she had been very observant.

"But," she said, "he would then point out the spider, a bee, a dead fly, and about twenty other things where I would see only one. So I learned to use my eyes."

The mountain gorilla has jet-black skin and dense, shiny black hair, longer than that of its lowland cousins. The males weigh up to five hundred pounds and stand six feet tall upright. The females are smaller. Gorillas are the largest primates and live only in the rain forests of equatorial Africa, high in the mountains that surround once-active volcanoes. No one knows how many of these magnificent animals once roamed the forests, but now there are only a few thousand left.

They wander during the day, feeding on fruits, nettles, snails, grubs, and leaves. They have few enemies—an occasional leopard and always man. The full-grown apes do not go swinging through the trees; they are too heavy and would break branches. But the youngsters do, making their nests in the trees at night, always in a different spot. The adults settle in nests on the ground or in low branches for the night and nap there in the midday heat.

Before Dian began the trip to the Virunga Mountains, she went home to California for a visit. She stopped at the Stanford Primate Facility to learn what was known about gorillas. Then she had her appendix out, just to avoid a possible emergency once she was in Africa. One of her first stops in Africa was at the Gombe Reserve to talk with Jane Goodall.

Then she headed for Zaire, one of three new nations born from the Belgian Congo. In a state of political unrest, these nations were not the safest place for a foreigner, and the border between Zaire and Uganda was already closed. But Dian went ahead. She did not have a two-way radio or any outside contact, but she never felt lonesome or isolated. She was content with her mission and eager to learn about the gorillas.

Following old elephant and buffalo trails, she set out to look for the animals. Locating them was no problem because their huge bodies left paths of broken and bent branches. But whenever she got close, the huge beasts would scream and run away as soon as the leader caught sight of her. She knew from Jane Goodall's experience how long it had taken to habituate the chimpanzees, and she saw no reason to think the intelligent gorillas would be different. So she was patient, and after a while they allowed her to sit and watch them. Sometimes she wondered who was the observer and who the observed.

Just as things were going well, the director of Virunga National Park decided he could not guarantee her safety, and he sent six guards to put her under house arrest. She was supposed to stay put. She didn't like that, so she took matters into her own hands. Convincing the guards that she had to register her car across the border, she got into closed Uganda and stayed there. She was without her supplies and equipment, but she had taken care to carry her valuable notes.

As soon as she got more supplies together, she set out for a new camp on Mount Visoke, only five miles from the old one. It was so far up the mountain that her old VW bus took her to the 8,000-foot mark, and she had to hike the next 2,000 feet to her cabin. Fortunately, the gorillas don't know anything about political borders, and she was able to watch many of the same groups.

Dian had the feeling that the gorillas were suspicious of anyone just sitting there and staring, so she began to imitate them. Her goal was to be among them and watch without changing their behavior. She would arrive so early in the morning that she also had the feeling that she had become the signal to the gorillas to "get up, it's morning."

She learned to fold her arms across her chest. It let the animals know she meant no harm. She assumed it was their sign for submission, because when she did it they went on feeding. She learned to scratch, to keep her head down, and to belch. She tasted their food and found that, if restless, gorillas would calm down when she reached out and picked some wild celery to munch. She said that she sometimes felt quite foolish sitting there alone in the wet drizzle of a mountain forest, thumping her chest rhythmically like the gorillas, chewing some wild plant. But it allowed her to be close, and that's what she wanted. After a few years, the gorillas became so used to this hairless ape that they poked into her knapsack, looked at her notebook, fussed with the laces of her boots, and handled her valuable camera with their big hands.

One day the park rangers brought her an infant gorilla that had been captured for a zoo in West Germany. The tiny thing was only half-alive. It had been in a cage for twenty-six days with little to eat except bananas. Although she was furious that it had been captured and hated the idea of its being sent to a zoo, she said she would care for it. Otherwise it would surely die. The rangers lugged it up the mountain trail to her sheet-metal cabin. It was in a child's play-pen with a top nailed on.

She had cleared out one room of the cabin, arranging it with leaves on the floor and a tree in one corner. Once out of the playpen, the baby zipped up the tree, only to be stopped by the ceiling.

He cried himself to sleep that first night, but gradually he responded to her loving care. She named him Coco. Another youngster arrived soon after, this one a two-year-old she named Puckerpuss, also destined for a zoo.

Her native cook quit because he refused to cook for apes, and Dian had to give up valuable gorilla-watching time to stay with the infants. But she learned a lot from the babies. She listened carefully to the sounds they made, the gentle *naoom naoom* and the little grunts of comfort. She took them outdoors and watched as they hunted for grubs and snails under tree bark. It was the first time she knew for certain that gorillas ate anything but the wild nettles, celery, and other plants so plentiful on the mountain.

One day when Dian was close to a group of gorillas, she imitated one of the noises she had learned from her babies, and she found it meant something like "come and get it . . . food is served" to a gorilla. The leader of the group walked over to her, saw that she did not have anything to eat, and gave her a look that clearly meant, "Come on now, you can't fool me."

She learned that the belch, which she could imitate well, expressed comfort and well-being, much as it does for humans after a huge meal. Dian once crawled quietly among a group of feeding gorillas and brought up a resounding belch. She was delighted when each of the animals around her answered her with its own belch.

A gentle pig-grunt is used by mothers to let their children know if all is well. A leader can stop a squabble in his group with a sharp grunt. He emits a loud whoop-bark to sound an alarm, and a roar when he is displaying and beating his chest. The chest-beating can be heard a great distance, and it seems to be the gorilla's way of releasing tension. It certainly upsets the enemy!

Dian collected hundreds of plants that the gorillas fed upon, but she did not see them drink. Apparently they get enough water from the plants they eat. And she did not see them make or use tools. Perhaps they have no need of them—they eat such a wide variety of food that it is easily available without working to get it.

As she learned to tell the individuals apart and began to name them, she also kept a photographic record. She took close-ups that showed the gorillas' noseprints. The noseprint is as unique to a gorilla as a fingerprint is to a human.

She found that the gorillas, unlike the chimps, do not gather in large communities, even to feed. A gorilla group is led by an adult male with white fur on his back. He is called a silverback. There are several adult females with their young, and a few younger males. They do not spend a lot of time grooming each other as the chimps do, but they do groom, carefully picking through their thick fur to find bits of dirt and dead skin.

Gorillas have no definite territory to defend, and they travel through a home range that crosses the paths of other gorillas. When they do meet, there is usually no problem, although different groups do try to avoid each other.

Dian found that the behavior of a group is usually related to the kind of leader it has. The gorillas in one group she knew were placid and relaxed. They did not get excited or move away when she joined them. Their leader was a calm old silverback that Dian named Whinny because he had a strange voice. When he died, another

Pucker Puss, a captive two-year-old female gorilla, and Coco, a sixteen-month-old male, enjoy a frolic with Dian Fossey. Watching gorillas in the wild, Ms. Fossey found adult males to be very protective and tolerant of the young. She once saw an old male tickle an infant with a flower, as might a kindly grandfather. Ms. Fossey observed the great apes under a grant from the National Geographic Society. (Photo by Robert M. Campbell, © National Geographic Society)

gorilla, Uncle Bert, became the leader, and the behavior of the group changed. Suddenly Dian was no longer accepted. When she appeared, the gorillas beat their chests and hit trees and made a lot of noise. Dian thought of Uncle Bert as a "cantankerous old goat."

One day as she watched this group, a small baby gorilla toddled over to Uncle Bert, who was resting. She expected him to be annoyed with the youngster, but instead he picked a flower and tickled the baby under the chin with it. He sat there, Dian reported, with "an idiotic grin on his face."

Gorillas fiercely defend their young. Dian once saw a young gorilla she named Icarus—a youngster she described as a "wizened, elf-eared little fellow"—playing in a tree when a branch broke and he crashed to the ground. The noise startled the adult gorillas, and the silverback leader led a charge toward Dian. "They came at me as if my presence had caused the mishap," she said.

They stopped about ten feet from her when they saw that Icarus was again climbing a tree, quite unhurt. "But they remained tense, giving frequent barks of alarm," she said. "Then to my dismay, a small infant climbed into the same broken sapling and began a series of spins, twirls, leg hangs, kicks and chest-pats. No high-wire artist ever had such a rapt audience."

The eyes of the silverback males glanced from Dian to the youngster, and they roared threateningly whenever their glances met. Finally, Icarus, who had started the whole thing, broke the tension by starting a game of tag with the acrobatic infant, leading him back to the group. The big males beat their chests a few times as if to get in the last word and then ran away. Dian was greatly relieved.

In the thousands of hours of actual watching, Dian can report seeing only a few minutes of behavior that could be called aggressive, and that was the time the five big males charged her and she shouted "Whoa." This was most likely a bluff, a reaction to being startled by the appearance of a different kind of ape.

These are gentle animals who love to play. The groups are not families, but seem to be made up of individuals who stay together because they enjoy each other's company.

One of the things Dr. Leakey urged Dian to learn more about was how the gorilla groups change to ensure a healthy population. There are, of course, the changes of births and deaths. And they had seen some of the lone males drop out of a group to wander a while and then start their own new groups. But not much else was known about how new blood, new genes, were brought into a gorilla group.

After years of watching, Dian has found out that the males take females from other groups. Males from one group do not leave their group to join another; they leave it only to begin one of their own. Many males do not seek to be leaders of a group but remain as lower-ranking males with an established group. But Dian knows that she will need years more of watching to really understand the transfer process. From what she knows so far, this transfer does not seem to be what she calls "economical"—that is, even though the groups change, they do not grow quickly because the silverback male, the leader, is likely to kill any infant belonging to a new female he takes into the group. Infants fathered by males in his group are, of course, a part of the group. But Dian says, "One does begin to wonder what the purpose of this is when they are trying to bring new blood in to breed while they are killing off young stock. I do not have the answer for this."

In recent years, Dian has seen cannibalism among the peaceful gorillas. She stopped watching one group for a while because they were too habituated, too friendly. When she picked up the contact again, she could not find one of the babies, Banjo. She looked everywhere and found not a trace. Finally, she and her helpers collected hundreds of pounds of gorilla dung. They sifted all of it and found in the waste of one female gorilla most of the bones of baby Banjo. So once more, there is a new question, a new puzzle. And always the question, *why?*

When asked about her long-range goals for the gorilla study, Dian said, "We are all there to continue our protection of the area." (She is referring to her graduate students, visiting scientists, and African helpers when she says "we.")

"Within the Virunga Mountains, there are only 269 gorillas left. Our study aims are census work, to do recounts, rechecks and continuing behavior studies. I think in terms of year to year."

After her first few years in the African mountains, Dian went to Cambridge University in England to work on a doctoral thesis. Just before she left, she had what she called "the most wonderful going-away present I could have had."

She was sitting near a group of gorillas she had known for several years, and one male, Peanuts, wandered near her. He began to show off, strutting around in front of her, beating his chest. To calm him, she used a gesture she had used many times before that seemed to reassure the animals. She raised one arm and began to scratch herself with the other arm. Peanuts did the same.

Then she held out her hand, palm up. Peanuts stood up, and for a moment he seemed uncertain as to what he should do next. Then he reached out and touched her gently with his enormous black hand. It was probably the first recorded friendly physical contact between a human and a 450-pound wild gorilla. Peanuts turned away, and he was so excited he raced off toward the others, beating his chest. It was such a thrilling moment for Dian Fossey that she couldn't help but cry—for joy.

Chapter Ten

Biruté Galdikas and the Red Apes

"I like being alone in the forest. It is slightly magical. The whole quality of the world changes when you're in the forest."

Biruté Galdikas could say that after the blood-bloated leeches had fallen out of her socks, dropped off her neck and squirmed out of her underwear. She could say that even after she had waded through waist-deep swampy water where crocodiles and poisonous snakes lived, even when her clothes and sneakers had rotted from the dampness and mildew. She could say that because she was where she wanted most to be, in the rain forests of Borneo learning the ways of the wild orangutans and teaching the "orange monster-babies" how to live free.

Biruté was a student at the University of California in Los Angeles in 1969 when Dr. Louis Leakey, who "found" Jane Goodall and Dian Fossey, visited there. She was majoring in anthropology, and her interest in human evolution led her to wonder about the least-known of the great apes, the orangutan. She was especially curious about why these apes lived alone when the other apes are social. She convinced Dr. Leakey that she was the right person to send to Indonesia for a long-term study of the red apes.

During the two years it took to find the money to support the study, Biruté worked on her graduate studies and learned more about the only one of the great apes in Asia. At one time there were half a million of them, extending into northern China. There are less than ten thousand in the world now, and that includes those captive in zoos and in research laboratories. Man is the orangutan's only enemy.

The orangutans are called *Pongo pygmaeus*. They are shy and slow-moving, and not much is known about the way they spend their solitary days. The females and males are easy to tell apart because they look quite different. The males weigh up to 250 pounds, twice the size of the female, and when they are twelve to fifteen years old they begin to develop large, fleshy cheek pads and a throat pouch that the females do not have. The throat pouch is probably a reso-nator for the orangutan's long-call, a cry Biruté describes as a "hair-raising, minutes-long sequence of roars and groans that carry a mile." It is also an astounding sound to hear for the first time in the still-ness of the rain forest.

Before the long study began, Biruté married Rod Brindamour, a physicist who became the orang project's administrator and photog-rapher. In 1971, they arrived in Borneo, now called Kalimantan, one of the islands of Indonesia. It is a hot, steamy land, lush with over-grown jungles and narrow, winding waterways. It is seldom cooler than ninety degrees, and there is hardly any dry season at all.

Dr. Leakey told Biruté, "I will give you ten years to make contact with the orangutans. If you don't do it in ten years I won't support you longer."

"Fortunately," said Biruté, "I began to learn very quickly."

Biruté and Rod traveled thirty miles to their first outpost, Camp Leakey, in a small ironwood dugout with their supplies. The camp was a bark-walled, thatch-roofed hut. It was difficult not to think about dry, clean beds, hot showers, ice cream cones, and other comforts left behind. But they became caught up in the excitement of the project so quickly that they were soon used to the new way of life.

The study area of Tanjung Puting Reserve is fourteen square miles. Rod hacked out miles and miles of trails through the forests that first year and made pathways through the *ladang*—dried-up rice paddies overgrown with ferns and grasses. The first day at the Reserve, Biruté and Rod saw an orangutan high in the trees.

In the Malaysian language, the word "orangutan" means "wild person of the forest." Its name may be a clue to its destruction. It is such a manlike creature, with a manlike face, and it is such a funny imitator of man's ways, that it has been used as a pet, an entertainer in circuses (billed as "The Wild Man of Borneo"), and an exhibit in zoos.

In ancient times, the ape was hunted for food, and it is said that some tribes in remote regions of Borneo still use the ape for meat. During the 1920's, Dutch animal dealers collected orangutans by chopping down trees to force the animals to retreat to a few isolated trees, where they could then be driven into nets or starved out. Many were killed in the process, of course, and many more died miserably in shipment. In one year, 102 Sumatran orangutans were sent to Europe. One American circus bought thirty-three of them.

Even when that kind of collecting stopped, trappers captured young animals for the pet trade by shooting the mothers. The little ones need almost as much care as human infants, and they are easily raised in a human family. Some of these red-haired babies were treated like spoiled children. They ate at their captors' tables and wore fancy jeweled collars and sometimes clothes. Others did not fare so well and were crammed into small cages or chained in yards.

In Indonesia and Malaysia, it is now illegal to own, kill, or export an orangutan. But poachers are still killing the mothers because they can always find someone who will pay a high price for the baby animals. The habitat of the orang is being destroyed by logging operations and land-clearing for agriculture. On its own, the orangutan doesn't have much chance of survival. The Indonesian Forestry Service has been confiscating captive orangutans, taking them from people who keep them as pets. They were delighted when Biruté and Rod set up their project, and they asked the young couple if they would act as a halfway house—a rehabilitation center where the orangutans could learn to be wild again. There are two other rehabilitation centers in Indonesia, one in Malaysian Borneo and the other in northern Sumatra. Theirs would serve Kalimantan.

Captive orangutans that were turned out into the forests would soon die. They would not know how to find food or protect themselves, and most were taken so young that they had not yet learned how to build a nest. Biruté and Rod thought the center was a great idea. What could be easier? And it would give them a chance to learn about the red apes first-hand.

"At first Rod and I had the idea that ex-captives would eagerly return to forest life," said Biruté. But they were in for a surprise with their "repossessed" animals.

Of all the great apes, orangs are the only ones that do not live in groups or some kind of social community. They have only short periods when they are with others of their kind—during courtship, mating, and some friendships when they are immature. The longest time they spend with others are the early years when the mother and young are together.

In camp, the orangutans were anything but solitary and unsocial. They had become so attached to humans and the easy life of civilization that Biruté and Rod literally had to drag them back to the forest. But they wouldn't stay.

Sugito was the first little orphan to become one of Biruté's babies. He was one year old and had been kept in a small crate before the authorities found him. When he climbed into Biruté's arms the first time, he decided she was his mother. If he had been raised in the forest, he would have been carried everywhere for at least a year and a half. He never let go of Biruté, not even when she went into the river for a bath or when she went to bed. When she tried to change her clothes with the little orang hugging her, he fought and howled as she shifted him from one side to the other.

It wasn't long before there was a houseful of babies. It was impossible to keep the animals outside the fragile hut. They even had one orang who poked her head right up through the thatch roof to see if it was still raining. And the animals took everything. At night, if

An orphan orangutan clutches the gunwales of a dugout paddled by Biruté Galdikas-Brindamour, who is observing the great apes in Borneo's rain forest. The young scientist, with her photographer husband, made the first long-range study of the apes, an endangered species. (Photo by Rod Brindamour, © National Geographic Society)

Biruté and Rod did not give them something to wrap up in or settle into for a substitute nest, they would bang around all night until they found something—clothes, blankets, anything.

The little "rehabs" loved to put things in their mouths—flashlight batteries, toothpaste, brushes. Biruté said that there was nothing without orang toothmarks on it. They tasted everything and ripped apart books, clothes, even an umbrella. Sugito loved to wait until Biruté wasn't looking and then spit a mouthful of chewed rice into her tea.

"I was sometimes convinced that they were using their high ape intelligence to maximum capacity just thinking up ways to drive us crazy. Cempaka would dump bowls of salt in my tea. Sobiarso would eat flashlight bulbs, and both she and Rio would suck all our fountain pens dry. I would find old socks in my morning coffee. It was a continual battle of wits, and they won!"

Biruté watched the wild orang mothers for clues to raising her orphans. She learned that "Help yourself" is the rule in the wild, too. Because the young orangs do not have to learn to play with other orangs or get along in a group, they do not need social rules. The babies may have temper tantrums when they want something the mother is eating, but the mother just waits until the baby is through screaming, paying little attention to the fuss. She does not hand the baby food. The baby takes it from her mouth and learns the taste of foods it can eat. Biruté and Rod collected two hundred different foods the orangs eat, including fruits, berries, leaves, bark, insects, and eggs. Biruté has never yet seen an orangutan eat meat. One of her orphans took a dead mouse away from a cat and examined it closely, but he threw it away with a look of disgust on his expressive face.

Gradually, the orphans learned to fend for themselves. In 1974, when their ape-proof house, complete with screens, was finally ready, Biruté and Rod moved in, leaving the other camp to the orangs. The apes had a great time tearing it apart, but they had to sleep in the forest as a result. Rod and Biruté often took the rehabs by the hand and walked them through the *ladang* paths into the trees. Rod spent hours one day showing a little orang how to bend branches to make a nest, but the orang just stared at him blankly.

Although Biruté felt a little sad when the orphans were finally ready to live in the forest, she also felt like a proud parent whose child has graduated from school.

Rod and Biruté continued their study of wild orangs even while they worked with the halfway house. They went out every day, walking the paths, listening. Sometimes the only clue to the whereabouts of an orang was the sound of twigs breaking or the sound of fruit pits dropping to the ground. Once in a while they would hear the crashing of branches as the orangs broke off limbs, some as big as logs, and sent them hurtling down as a warning.

Throatpouch was the first male orang who allowed Biruté and Rod near. They had been following him constantly for two weeks, and they had known him for about two months when they realized that he had accepted them. Throatpouch was in a tree, and Rod and Biruté were sitting below, resting, when suddenly the big male came down the trunk of the tree and looked at them.

Biruté said, "I thought, well, it's all over. It's finished. We're going to be attacked." But he just totally ignored them, turned his back on them and began eating the termites that he had dug up with his claws.

Biruté began to learn the pattern of the orangs' day. She charted their pathways, learned what territories were inhabited by whom, and began to see some relationships. She was no longer surprised to see the big orangs walking on the ground; they are so heavy that ground travel is easier. The big males often make simple nests on the ground, especially for their afternoon rest. They go into the fifty- and sixty-foot high betel palms and ironwoods mainly to eat and sleep.

Orangutan hands are specially adapted for swinging on branches. The fingers are long and can hook securely around a limb. The thumb is short and stubby and stays out of the way when the ape swings. The young orangs and lighter females swing from limb to limb, but when a tree is far away, they swing the branch they are on and use it like a pendulum to leap to the next tree.

Biruté found that the females travel about six miles a day in their home range, but it is not a private territory. They often met other females traveling with their young, or adolescent females feeding together for a while. She saw young orangs play together for short periods and sometimes even groom each other, but they were all short contacts, and when the animals were sexually mature they no longer played together.

Biruté says her most vivid memory is of the time she came face to face with a large adult male on the ground. It was a scorching-hot day. She was walking along a path through a *ladang* when she saw a huge orangutan ambling along, head down, paying no attention to anything. Suddenly he stopped in his tracks, less than twelve feet from her. For many seconds they stared at each other. Biruté described the scene: "I guess he was evaluating the bizarre sight in front of him—a pale-faced primatologist with large black sunglasses, clutching an enormous bag full of dirty laundry."

There was nowhere to go. The narrow path was fenced in by tall ferns that almost closed in overhead like a tunnel. "But strangely, I felt no fear," Biruté said. "I simply marveled at how magnificent he looked with his coat blazing orange in the full sunlight."

Then he whirled away abruptly and padded back down the trail.

Although she had been surprised to meet an orang on the path, she was no longer surprised to see a big male on the ground after having known Nick.

Nick was a male they had followed from dawn to dusk for sixty-four days. They were determined never to let him out of their sight. When he built his nest for the night, they rested or returned to camp if it was not too far, and they were at the nest site by dawn when Nick awoke.

On the forty-fifth day of following Nick, they saw him looking for termites, and they had a moment that Biruté said she hardly dared hope for. Nick broke off a piece of wood, which they thought he might use as a tool, as the chimps did. But he only examined it closely, looking for termites, before he threw it down.

Biruté and Rod sat down on the end of the log where Nick was feeding. Suddenly, Nick stopped eating and swung around to look at the intruders. He stood upright and moved toward them until he was only a few feet away. Biruté and Rod did not move. They kept their heads down, their eyes away from Nick's. Direct eye contact is a sure sign of aggression among the apes. They waited. Slowly, Nick dropped to a crouch again. Still they waited. After what seemed like forever, Nick moved back to his end of the log and began to poke around again for termites. He was truly habituated. Rod and Biruté were part of his daily life.

Years later, Nick showed them another difference between orangs and the other apes. One day they watched as he waded out into the shallow lake near the camp and munched on reeds growing near the shore. Biruté says it took four years to see this because Nick was not secure enough with them to leave the safe tropical rain forest for the more open area of the lake.

Chimps and gorillas avoid the water whenever they can. They step across streams. But the orang's habitat has so many waterways that they have adapted to it, although they do not swim. Like the other apes, they do not like the rain; but unlike the chimps and gorillas, who sit in misery in the rain, the orangs do something about it. They build platforms over their nests and often sleep, dry and comfortable, through the long afternoon rains. If they don't have time to build a roof, they hold large leaves like umbrellas over themselves.

Biruté has come to understand the three distinct units of orangutan society—the mothers and infants, the adolescents, and the solitary males. The old males are often seen with bent or broken toes and fingers. Biruté and Rod watched fights between adult males, which probably accounted for some of the deformities of the animals. But they have also seen these animals fall from the trees, and certainly they have broken bones from that.

The orangutans are intelligent animals. Those in the halfway house used household tools all the time. One day a female watched Biruté make pancakes. Then she grabbed a glass, a handful of flour, a handful of sugar, and some eggs, put them all together, and beat them with a spoon. The orangs often used sticks to poke at things, and little Sugito would bring Biruté a cherished bottle of Coca-Cola and an opener. She knew exactly what the opener did.

Biruté thought that perhaps the abundance of food, along with not having to share it with a community, explained why the orangutans never learned to make or use primitive tools. But that was only a few years into the study. After five and a half years, Biruté saw an orangutan break off a dead branch and use it as a back scratcher. "Certainly, this was not a very dramatic instance of tool use," she told a group when she was lecturing in the United States, "but it was, nonetheless, tool use."

Biruté and Rod have learned a lot about the life of the red apes, and how their habitat in the Asian rain forests has been responsible for adaptations different from those of their African relatives. But they know that there is more that they have yet to learn.

"A five-and-a-half-year study such as ours represents only a good beginning when one is dealing with long-lived complex primates such as orangutans," Biruté explains. Orangs have lived to the age of fifty-seven years in captivity.

But Biruté and Rod have been studying orangutans long enough to begin to see the relationships between generations of these animals. They have watched an older female orang they know to be the grandmother of one of the youngsters, and they expect to learn much from these animals. They have not witnessed the aggression and cannibalism seen in the gorillas and chimps, except with a once-captive orang they did not consider normal. So there is much more study ahead, and many more questions to answer. Like the other animal watchers, they agree that the more they find out, the more questions they learn to ask.

Biruté and Rod's young son now shares their life in the Tanjung Puting Reserve. They have Indonesian students learning to watch the wild apes, and they hope to have a permanent field station one day, a place where other animals of the rain forest will be studied, a place the Indonesian people themselves can develop should Biruté and Rod be forced to discontinue their work there.

The "wild person of the forest" is not so much a mystery as he once was.

Chapter Eleven

Leone Pippard, Heather Malcolm, and the Sea Canaries

As the small inflated rubber boat putt-putted downriver, Heather Malcolm zipped up her black wet suit and adjusted her face mask. Her partner, Leone Pippard, cut the motor, and the boat drifted. Hesitating just a minute to look around and make sure she wouldn't land on a whale, Heather jumped into the near-freezing water, clutching her underwater camera.

She knew at once why the white whales that swam fifteen feet from the boat were called sea canaries. She was bombarded with noise—whistling, singsong sighing, grunting, barking, chirping, clicking—the sounds the whales use to find food and keep in touch with each other.

A clanking noise came from the boat, and instantly the whale sounds stopped. Whales have extremely good hearing. In the dark ocean water, where they cannot see food or friends and enemies, they must find them by sound. They send out sound waves that bounce back to them like an echo, telling them the size and shape of the thing they are "looking" at. It is a complicated system of communication that scientists are only beginning to understand.

Whales can also sort out a continuous hodgepodge of noises. If three radios are playing at once, you probably would not be able to understand any of them. Most humans can receive only one message at a time. But a whale can be sending out his own signals at the same time he is receiving messages from every other whale in the area.

These white whales are commonly called belugas. The name came from the Russian word "byely," which means "white," and a white whale is "byelukha." There is also a huge, white fish, the sturgeon, called a "beluga" in Russia. Somehow the rhyming words got confused, as names often do, and now almost everyone, including Russian scientists, calls the happy-looking white whales "belugas."

The home range of these whales is the entire Arctic Ocean. Many of them migrate to more temperate waters following the Arctic codfish, which they like to eat. Cod travel by the millions in schools. Whale travel in smaller groups called pods.

One large pod of belugas feeds in the Gulf of St. Lawrence, where that great river empties into the Atlantic Ocean. That is where Heather Malcolm and Leone Pippard first met Ole Ivory, Karen, Fat, Robin, William, and the ninety-five other belugas they named.

Heather and Leone had never heard of beluga whales when they met as students at the Ontario College of Art in Toronto in 1968. Neither had taken any science courses, except for basic biology in high school. But they were to discover that their skills in photography and writing would make it possible for them to study whales.

In 1973, Heather was teaching photography when she heard that Project Jonah, an international organization trying to save whales from becoming extinct, was hiring young students to set up continuous watches along the St. Lawrence to count and identify whales.

"Let's go," Heather said to Leone. "It would make a great story for a magazine. We'll photograph the whales and the watchers and write about them."

But Leone was not particularly interested. She had a good job as a rent control investigator at the time, and she had not given much thought to whales.

Finally Heather gave Leone a book. "Here, read this," she said. "Maybe it will explain things better than I can."

Leone began to read *A Whale for the Killing* by Farley Mowatt, a Canadian author and naturalist. It is the sad but true story of a stranded whale that dies because no one will help. Before the end of the last chapter, Leone called Heather. "Let's go," she said.

During the next few months they begged, borrowed, and bought equipment and supplies. A friend loaned them a camper to travel and live in. An oil company gave them a credit card for free gas, and another firm loaned them an underwater movie camera. They took all their personal savings and headed for Quebec.

They arrived at the Saguenay River on a cold day. A drizzling rain was falling, and fog hung like a gray curtain, blotting out all scenery. They could not even find the Bay of St. Marguerite in the Saguenay River, where they were supposed to meet the Project Jonah people.

Speaking only schoolbook French, they had a difficult time renting a boat from a French-speaking seaman. Their camper got stuck in wet sand, and while they worked to free it, they were so badly bitten by black flies and mosquitoes that they almost went crazy. Heather jumped into a small dark pool to escape the insects, only to come up covered with slimy sewage.

Exhausted and discouraged, they finally parked the muddy camper on a wharf and crawled into their sleeping bags. Just as they were falling asleep, a blast from a foghorn sent them leaping from their bunks, colliding in midair. In the dark they had parked under a foghorn that moaned its message to ships all night. If there had been an easy way to return home right then, Heather and Leone would probably have taken it. But there was nothing to do but wait for dawn.

On the second day they woke to bright sunlight. After a quick breakfast, they opened the camper door and studied the area. Sun sparkled on the waves of the river. There was no wind, but great whitecaps rolled endlessly by. And then they realized that the whitecaps were whales—hundreds of belugas surfacing, blowing, rolling back down in a great, steady rhythm.

Heather said her heart pounded as though it would break out of her chest. Goose bumps chilled her. "There is no way to describe the thrill of seeing these beautiful creatures for the first time. We were not prepared for their grace and calm, their lustrous whiteness."

But the belugas were only one of many exciting surprises that first day. In their haste to get the boat launched and keep their eyes on the whales at the same time, cameras and scuba gear got dropped and stepped on, but finally stowed in the boat and the boat in the water.

When the boat was well out into the current, they turned off the motor and drifted. The whales did not seem to mind the putt-putting of the motor; they stayed nearby, sometimes coming within a foot or two of the boat, as long as the motor just trolled along. But when it speeded up, the whales disappeared.

The whales either followed the boat or swam parallel to it, but they did not seem to like it when the boat followed them. It may be that their sonar did not work as well when they were not facing the object they wanted to hear. Or it may have been some leftover wariness from the days when the belugas were hunted in great numbers by early Canadian settlers and Eskimos. They continuously turned their heads, like people hard of hearing who are trying to stay with a conversation.

At first, Heather and Leone worried about being capsized by the large animals. But the whales were never aggressive. They never approached the boat quickly or rushed at it.

In the midst of the white whales there suddenly appeared a hulking body, coming directly toward the boat. Leone and Heather hung on to the sides of the boat. What was this monstrous creature? Would it ram the boat?

It was a fin whale, one of the giants of the sea—an eighty-foot mammal rising and diving, paying no attention to the small belugas. As Heather and Leone watched, the beautiful whale passed so close to the boat that they could almost touch its broad back.

Perhaps it was the lush plankton bloom, a growth of microscopic plants and animals that baleen whales gulp down by the ton, that brought the whales into the bay that day, for soon after they saw

Leone Pippard and Heather Malcolm sitting in their small boat from which they study whales.

more. A second fin whale passed, and then a thirty-foot minke, a sixty-foot sei, and, most incredible of all, four blue whales. These are the largest animals ever to live on this planet, larger than any of the great dinosaurs. They grow to be one hundred feet long, and now they are almost extinct. But there they were.

"A blue surfaces and blows like a geyser," said Leone, "and it rolls by so gently, so gracefully and quickly that you suddenly realize it is a quarter of a mile downriver and you have not caught your breath."

During those few weeks in Quebec, Heather and Leone took reams of notes and dozens of pictures. They talked with conservation officers and government officials, and they watched the oil slicks on the river. They agreed that they would return to learn all they could about whales and their environment.

They went back to Toronto to make plans and find money for this long-term study. In the fall of 1974, they went to New York City to try to interest the New York Zoological Society in financing part of the study. They got no money, but they did meet Alex.

Alex was a 2,000-pound beluga whale who had lived at the New York Aquarium for thirteen years, and Heather and Leone were invited to enter his world.

They put on wet suits, masks, and fins and slipped into the fifty-two-degree water. At first Alex ignored them. They tried not to shiver or move, and they did not force a meeting.

"We both had the feeling that we were invading his home and that he would check us out when he was ready," Leone remembered.

Alex moved toward them slowly, nudging each of them gently, testing their flippers with his, poking at them with his ever-smiling face.

"Floating there with Alex, we became aware of how different is the world of the whale, how living in water makes you aware of your own internal self. You are very conscious of your heart beating, your every breath. You *hear* everything. You become aware of the currents that go by your body, the slightest changes," Leone continued.

Most of what is known about whales was learned from dead animals or from the few that are in captivity, like Alex. There are books that tell the size and shape and weight of every part of a whale's body. You can read how big a whale's lungs are or how thick the blubber is. You can find out how much an unborn whale baby weighs or what is in a whale's stomach. But no one really knows what a whale's life is like in the deep ocean.

It is wet and cold and uncomfortable to watch whales, but by this time Heather and Leone were so committed to whales that they did not care about cold or discomfort. On their return to Toronto, they began a full-scale campaign to find backing for their study.

"We sat on a park bench," said Heather, "our outdoor, rent-free office, and composed letters to every person and organization we could think of."

"We quite frankly used the fact," Heather continued, "that we were young women who looked nothing like anyone's idea of 'whaling women.' We hoped, of course, that the whales' problems would be enough to make people concerned. But we thought that if all other approaches failed, just the novelty of two young women doing something unusual might stir people into action. We didn't care *why* they gave us support, as long as they gave. It may not have been the scientific approach, but it worked."

"I called on the executive of a food company," said Heather, "and he was interested in whales."

"What do you need?" he asked.

"Raisins, oatmeal . . ." Heather began to read the list.

"Uh, well," he stammered, sinking behind his huge desk. "I don't think we can provide that, but I'll see what I can do."

When his donation arrived, there was enough jello to turn the entire Saguenay River into pudding. But little by little, more help arrived.

In the spring of 1975, Heather and Leone quit their jobs, loaded their camper, and headed for Quebec. And once again the beginning was bad.

They lost three weeks of their study when the boat they carried on top of the camper blew off and shattered. They waited in Quebec City for a new boat, and while they waited they practiced speaking French and learned about belugas and whaling history.

The belugas are one of two members of an ancient family of Arctic whales. The other is the narwhal, the whale with the long, swirled tusk that makes it look like a mythical sea unicorn. They are both toothed whales and have rows of peglike teeth that help them to catch fish. The larger whales, called the baleen whales, have plates of baleen, or bone, in their upper jaws through which they strain out the tons of minute animals they eat.

The male belugas average fifteen feet in length and may weigh up to two tons. The females are slightly smaller. The calves are slate-gray when they are born, and they whiten as they grow. Heather and Leone found that the belugas of the St. Lawrence area are actually blue in color when they are born.

These whales are not as athletic as the killer whales you see in oceanariums leaping through hoops and taking their trainers for rides. The belugas cannot make spectacular leaps because they are wrapped in heavy layers of blubber for warmth, and they do not make deep dives because they lack the large lung capacity of the larger whales. Unfortunately, belugas are easy to kill because they are small and don't dive deeply.

The beluga whales gather at ice holes, called savassats, making it easy to slaughter great numbers of them at one time. The meat and blubber have always been important winter rations for the Eskimos. The skin is tanned into "porpoise hide" and made into boots and boot laces. The bone is carved into souvenirs for the tourists.

The belugas provided a major industry for the Canadian fishermen in the 1930's, when there was still a commercial whale "fishery" and a bounty paid for killing the animals. A man could earn forty-five dollars for presenting the fluke—part of the triangular tail of a whale—to the proper official. Even when the bounty was lowered, there were more than five hundred belugas killed in the St. Lawrence region out of a population of two or three thousand. It is estimated that there are only five hundred belugas left in the entire St. Lawrence Bay today. In 1939, the whaling station died of its own greed.

Heather and Leone's first venture had taught them something about the general movements of an entire pod of whales. On their second trip to the St. Lawrence, paid for once again by small dona-tions from industry and government, the young women concentrated their studies on individual animals and small groups.

They were able to identify one hundred individual whales on this trip. They named each one, often by its markings. There was William, for example, who was named for the definite W shape on the back, and Gouge, an old male who had a huge gash, or gouge, in his skin. Some animal naturalists tag animals in order to identify them, but Heather and Leone did not find that necessary. Although the whales all looked alike the first day, it soon became apparent that there were many differences between them.

They kept careful records, using drawings on a clipboard to indi-cate the individual whales and a tape recorder to tell about the be-havior they saw. During the first few days, when they were still excited by the novelty of the work, they sometimes forgot to turn on the tape machine, but they soon became careful watchers.

They learned that Robin was the leader. It was he who always checked out their boat first. Some of the belugas were shy, but others could not seem to hide their curiosity. At the beginning of the summer, many of them swam near the boat as though investigat-ing, but toward the end of the summer, they seemed bored and paid little attention when Heather and Leone showed up.

One day when the young women were puttering down the river, they thought they saw a large piece of plastic foam floating ahead. As they approached slowly, the object did not move. They turned off the motor and drifted. For eight minutes they watched the floating body, until they finally realized that it was a sleeping beluga. When the animal awoke, it looked at them for a moment and then sub-merged.

"We were forever interrupting their sleep," said Leone.

When the belugas sleep they float near the surface, breathing slowly. In the mornings Heather and Leone took the boat into a shallow bay where they could see two or three of the white animals resting. In a matter of minutes there were belugas all around the boat. "And they did not arrive from anywhere," said Leone. "They were just there, submerged, resting."

They seemed to rest on beds of kelp at low tide when the water was only three feet deep.

Belugas, and probably most whales, have no definite territory marked by boundaries, as land animals do. Their boundary is the extent of the water. They go where the food is. And they are not fussy eaters. They like herring, flounder, sea trout, cod, and smelt, but if those supplies are low, they will eat worms and crustaceans from the river bottom.

A large group of belugas feeds together on the incoming tide and then splits into smaller groups. Ten or twenty females with a nursery of young make up one group. Another group with thirty to forty males, and perhaps some older females, gathers to move in another direction. This group of males sometimes splits into subgroups of five or ten animals, taking with them a young animal, one whose skin has not lost its blue-gray color. If one group of animals meets another during the day, they circle, as many animals do, then go their separate ways. After the daily separation, the entire pod gathers together again to feed and rest and sleep.

As Heather and Leone were chugging along one day, observing one of the groups of females and young, an older whale they had named Ole Ivory surfaced just a foot from the boat. Ole Ivory's left eye was clouded over by a cataract. She was stiff and slightly sway-backed. She poked her head out of the water, stared at the young women for a minute with her good right eye, and then settled next to the boat, staying close for at least an hour.

"We had the feeling that she was in control of the situation, that she was observing us. No doubt we did look strange, what with our black wet suits, and cameras like protruding eyes, and the constant hum of the motor. We enjoyed her trust. We both felt that she could quite rightly check us out," said Leone.

In the hours that Heather and Leone watched, they saw not one sign of aggression—not toward them, the boat, or even toward other whales. But the animals did discipline their young. One day two young calves were diving, darting, dashing at each other, biting at each other's tails. The mother, swimming nearby, did not seem to mind until one of the calves nipped her tail. She gave a great squawk, like a cat, and she batted the youngster head-on. After that, both young whales settled down to quieter play.

Heather and Leone made some of their observations from a helicopter, but that was too expensive to use as often as they would have liked. The bird's-eye view gave them an idea of how and where the pod moved, and how the whales fed. Based on views from the helicopter, Heather and Leone think that one beluga may go off to feed while several others dive to drive the fish toward the feeder. They have already made plans to spend many hours aloft, next time from hot-air balloons tethered over areas where the whales congregate.

There are so many things to be learned from watching whales. Heather and Leone want to study social relationships within a family, or within the pod. The feeding habits can help them determine how many whales can feed successfully in an area and how that, in turn, might affect the reproduction rate.

Their real dream is to establish a marine sanctuary in the Bay of St. Lawrence, a place where whales can safely survive and thrive, a place where people can go whale watching. Oil slicks, industry, and public wharves for recreation are all making it less possible for whales to survive. There is evidence that the St. Lawrence belugas do not migrate but remain in the bay all year. Lighthouse keepers have seen the animals there as late as December 15, when the keepers leave their posts for the winter freeze.

With the backing of the natural resources departments of the Canadian government and several corporations, Heather Malcolm and Leone Pippard will return to Quebec to continue watching. They hope to find the one hundred animals they identified and named, and this time to follow one small group for months. To know an individual whale as Jane Goodall knows Flo and Fifi, or as Kay McKeever knows Wheeper or Tiglet, may be impossible. The territory is different. But they are going to try.

Chapter Twelve

Is Animal Watching
for You?

Animal watching is not an ordinary job, and it is not for ordinary people. It is a way of life. The people who do become involved with the lives of animals find that it is not a job that runs from nine in the morning to five in the afternoon.

But if you are interested in such a job, there are ways in which you can prepare yourself.

After reading the stories of these women and their animals, you know that not all of them began with a college education. Some, in fact, had no training in zoology at all. But while you are still in school, it would be a good idea to take as many science courses as you can. Even if you don't study animals after all, the things you learn will never be wasted. An education is the one thing that can never be lost.

Take a basic biology course. Chemistry is generally required if you plan to go on to college science. Many high schools now offer courses in animal behavior, anatomy, physiology, or animal husbandry. Take as many as fit into your schedule.

But beyond school courses, there are some practical things that you should know.

DEVELOP YOUR WRITING SKILLS. That may sound like a strange thing to do if you want to watch animals, but it is important. Each of the women described in this book wrote about her experiences. Some wrote scientific papers, others wrote popular books, and some wrote both. Most of them also wrote grant requests.

It is often necessary to find financial support for a full-time job working with animals. A grant request is a written report describing exactly what you intend to study, what you hope to find out, and why it is important.

You should be able to write clearly enough to convince someone who knows nothing about animals that your work will be vital. You must be able to make them see how exciting the results will be, and how necessary. Writing will serve you in two ways—first, to help you find the money, but even more important, as a way to tell others what you have seen and learned.

PHOTOGRAPHY IS ANOTHER SKILL YOU MAY NEED. It is not enough for you to sit and watch an animal—except for your own enjoyment, of course. But if you hope to have your work count, if you hope to teach others about your animal, you must have records on film.

You can usually take basic photography at your school or the YMCA, YWCA, 4H Club, or similar organization. If none of these is available, ask a photographer in your area to teach you as an apprentice. And of course, there is the do-it-yourself method, which you can start by going to the library for books on beginning photography.

LEARN SOME MECHANICAL SKILLS. Can you fix a flat tire or put in a new spark plug? It may not be important in your life now, but it would be if you found yourself stranded in a desert with an ailing jeep. If your school offers a course in basic auto mechanics, take it. If it doesn't, ask where you can find one.

Whenever you have the opportunity, learn how to cope with the equipment at hand. Can you start an outboard motor? Can you operate a tape recorder or a gasoline camp stove?

FIRST AID. What would you do if you were miles into the wilderness and you found your foot was infected? Learn how to cope with such situations before you need to. Take a first-aid course.

Even if you never work in the field with animals, not one of these skills will ever be wasted. Every one of them makes you more self-reliant.

Each of the women in this book came from a different background, had different interests, received different educations. But there are some traits they did have in common.

All of them showed a great respect for life, an enormous amount of curiosity, a great deal of patience, a sense of adventure, a sense of wonder, and a love for animals. Each was a self-sufficient person who could be content to work alone. You can develop some of those traits, too.

Begin with the animals at hand. If you have pets, take full responsibility for them. Having someone else feed and groom the dog or clean the hamster cage is not a good way to begin a life with animals. There will be many difficult and dirty jobs. You don't have to smile while you do them, but don't grumble. Just do them.

If you live on a ranch or a farm, you have a head start, and you probably know a lot about animals. You may have a special relationship with an animal you have watched grow up, an animal you can "read" almost as though it can talk to you.

But if you live in the city, you may have to find places where you can be with animals. Volunteer to take care of the small animals in your school science department. If you take on that job, do it well. Never skip a day because you would rather go home early. Never ask someone to fill in for you unless you know that person will really do a good job. Animals in cages are totally dependent upon their human keepers for food, water, and cleanliness.

If your city has a zoo or an aquarium, volunteer to help clean cages or paint signs or whatever they will let you do. You will learn a great deal just being among the animals regularly. If there is a science museum or nature center in your city, they might have small animals in their education departments that need care.

Apply for a job with a veterinarian or in a pet shop. Offer to clean cages, or groom or exercise the animals.

OUTWARD BOUND. One of the most exciting ways to develop the self-reliance you will want to have is by taking part in Outward Bound or a similar program. These programs last from two to six weeks and teach you survival skills in the outdoors. You learn to handle all sorts of emergencies. In fact, during the final "test," you are left alone for a day or two in the wilderness with only basic supplies. How you survive depends upon not only the things you have learned about fire-making and compasses, but upon your own confidence. Some of these programs are expensive, but you can ask about scholarships.

The Student Conservation Corps has a volunteer program each summer for high school students who want to work in national parks. Local school districts are also beginning to offer courses in outdoor survival skills.

Although not everyone can be, or even wants to be, an animal watcher in the wilderness, each of us can watch over the animals. We can refuse to wear fur coats. We can support laws that prevent the hunting of animals that are endangered. We can support laws that set up wildlife preserves and that work toward better zoos.

The more people populate the earth, the more animals are squeezed out of their habitats. The earth would be a strange and uninteresting planet without its animal life. The more we know about animals and their relationships to us and the earth, the more likely we are to protect them. An extinct animal is gone forever. It can never live again.

We, too, are animals. If we cannot prevent the extinction of the other animals, how will we keep our own kind from becoming extinct?

Bibliography

Allen, Thomas B., ed. *The Marvels of Animal Behavior.* Washington, D.C.: National Geographic Society, 1972.

Benchley, Belle. *My Life in a Man-made Jungle.* Boston: Little, Brown and Co., 1940.

————. *My Friends the Apes.* Boston: Little, Brown and Co., 1942.

————. *My Animal Babies.* Boston: Little, Brown and Co., 1945.

Bergen, Candice. "With Jane Goodall in Africa." *Ladies Home Journal,* Feb. 1975, pp. 32–36.

Bourne, Geoffrey H., and Cohen, Maury. *The Gentle Giants: The Gorilla Story.* New York: G. P. Putnam's Sons, 1975.

Bridges, William. *Gathering of Animals.* New York: Harper & Row, 1974.

————. *Zoo Careers.* New York: William Morrow and Co., 1971.

Buyukmichi, Hope Sawyer, and Fantel, Hans. *Unexpected Treasure.* New York: M. Evans and Co., 1968.

————. *The Hour of the Beaver.* Chicago: Rand McNally and Co., 1971.

————. *Beaver Defenders* (newsletter), Nov.–Dec. 1975.

Cameron, Angus, and Parnall, Peter. *The Nightwatchers.* New York: Four Winds Press, Scholastic Book Services, 1971.

Carrighar, Sally. *Wild Heritage.* Boston: Houghton Mifflin Co., 1965.

Clark, Eugenie. *The Lady and the Sharks.* New York: Harper & Row, 1969.

————. *Lady with a Spear.* New York: Harper & Row, 1953.

————. "Mating of Groupers." *Natural History Magazine,* June 1965.

————. "Red Sea's Garden of Eels." *National Geographic,* Nov. 1972.

————. "The Red Sea's Sharkproof Fish." *National Geographic,* Nov. 1974, pp. 718–727.

————. "Into the Lairs of Sleeping Sharks." *National Geographic,* April 1975, pp. 571–584.

Cohen, Daniel. *Watchers in the Wild.* Boston: Little, Brown and Co., 1971.

Everett, Michael. *A Natural History of Owls.* London: Hamlyn Co., 1977.

Fossey, Dian. "Making Friends with Mountain Gorillas." *National Geographic,* Jan. 1970.

———. "More Years With Mountain Gorillas." *National Geographic,* Oct. 1971.

Galdikas-Brindamour, Biruté. "Orangutans, Indonesia's People of the Forest." *National Geographic,* Oct. 1974.

Gorner, Peter. "Ape Girls Get Along Without Tarzan." *Buffalo Evening News,* August 7, 1976, p. 7.

Hahn, Emily. *Animal Gardens.* New York: Doubleday and Co., 1967.

———. *On the Side of the Apes.* New York: Thomas Y. Crowell Co., 1971.

Harkness, Ruth. *The Lady and the Panda.* New York: Carrick & Evans, 1938.

———. *Pangoan Diary.* New York: Creative Age Press, 1942.

Harrison, Barbara. *Orangutans.* New York: Doubleday and Co., 1963.

Hornaday, W. T. *The Minds and Manners of Wild Animals.* New York: Charles Scribner's Sons, 1922.

Kevles, Bettyann. *Watching the Wild Apes. The Primate Studies of Goodall, Fossey, and Galdikas.* New York: E. P. Dutton and Co., 1976.

L. S. B. Leakey Foundation News. "The Great Apes, A Dialogue with Jane Goodall, Dian Fossey, Biruté Galdikas-Brindamour." No. 6, Fall 1976. A report of interviews on May 5, 1976, at the Foundation.

Linden, Eugene. *Apes, Men and Language.* New York: E. P. Dutton and Co., 1962.

Livingston, Bernard. *Zoo (Animals, People and Places).* New York: Arbor House Publishing Co., 1974.

MacKinnon, John. *In Search of the Red Apes.* New York: Holt, Rinehart and Winston, 1974.

McCarthy, J. D. *Animals and Their Ways: The Science of Animal Behavior.* New York: Natural History Press, 1965.

McIntyre, Joan, ed. *Minds in the Water.* New York: Charles Scribner's Sons, 1974.

Morris, Ramona and Desmond. *Men and Pandas.* New York: McGraw Hill, 1966.

Norris, Kenneth S. *The Porpoise Watcher.* New York: W. W. Norton and Co., 1974.

———. "Open Ocean Diving Test with a Trained Porpoise." *Deep Sea Research,* 12 (1965), pp. 505–509.

Perry, Richard. *The World of the Giant Panda*. New York: Taplinger Publishing Co., 1969.

Poling, James. *Beavers, Their Extraordinary Lives and Curious History*. New York: Franklin Watts, 1975.

Pryor, Karen. *Lads Before the Wind*. New York: Harper & Row, 1975.

————, Haag, Richard, and O'Reilly, Joseph. "The Creative Porpoise: Training for Novel Behavior." *Journal of the Experimental Analysis of Behavior*, 12 (1969), pp. 653–661.

Riedman, Sarah, and Gustafson, Elton. *Home Is the Sea for Whales*. Chicago: Rand McNally and Co., 1966.

Schaller, George. *The Year of the Gorilla*. Chicago: University of Chicago Press, 1964.

Scott, Jack Denton. "A Gentle Giant After All." *National Parks Magazine*, Nov. 1974, pp. 20–23.

Tinbergen, Niko. *Animal Behavior*. New York: Time-Life Books, 1970.

Van Lawick-Goodall, Jane. *My Friends the Wild Chimpanzees*. Washington, D.C.: National Geographic Society, 1967.

————. *In the Shadow of Man*. Boston: Houghton Mifflin Co., 1971.

————. "New Discoveries Among Africa's Chimpanzees." *National Geographic*, Dec. 1965, pp. 802–831.

Wilsson, Lars. *My Beaver Colony*. New York: Doubleday and Co., 1968.

In addition to the sources listed above, information was obtained from personal interviews, public speeches, and two films distributed by the National Geographic Society, Washington, D.C. 20036: "Miss Goodall and the Wild Chimpanzees" and "In Search of the Great Apes."

Organizations to Help You Learn about Animal Watching

BEAVERS
Beaver Defenders
Unexpected Wildlife Refuge, Inc.
Newfield, New Jersey 08344

THE APES
L. S. B. Leakey Foundation
Foundation Center 206–85
Pasadena, California 91125

WHALES AND PORPOISES
Project Jonah   Project Jonah, Canada
Box 476   or   12 Dakotah Ave.
Bolinas, California 94924   Toronto, Canada

Outward Bound, Inc.
165 W. Putnam Ave.
Greenwich, Connecticut 06830

Earthwatch
10 Juniper Rd.
Box 127
Belmont, Massachusetts 02178

Student Conservation Assoc., Inc.
P.O. Box 550
Charlestown, New Hampshire 03603

American Association of Zoos and Aquariums
Oglebay Park
Wheeling, West Virginia 26003
(Career Booklet)

Index

Adamson, Joy, 58
Africa, 40, 41, 42, 49, 53, 94, 95
Ailuropoda melanoleuca (giant
    panda), 28–29, 31, 32, 33–38
Akamai (spinner), 77
Alex (beluga), 118
Alpha male in chimpanzee commu-
    nity, 46–47, 48
American Association of Zoos and
    Aquariums, 133
Animal watching as a career, 124–127
    educational requirements for, 85,
        86, 124–125
    and a knowledge of first aid, 126
    mechanical skills needed for, 125–
        126
    organizations helpful in learning
        about, 133
    photography skills needed for, 125
    writing skills needed for, 125
Anthropoid apes, 42
Anthropomorphic thinking, 12
Apes, anthropoid, 42
Aquarium, New York, 118
Arctic Ocean, 114

Baboons, 16, 17, 18
Banjo (gorilla), 101
Bay of St. Lawrence, 123
Beaver Defenders, 71, 133
Beavers, 12, 13, 14, 61–71
    as dam and lodge builders, 69
    fossil bones of, 67

fur of, 68, 70
size of, 67
Behavior patterns, 14
Bei-shung (giant panda), 28–29, 31,
    32, 33–38
Belgian Congo, 22, 95
Belugas. *See* White whales
Benchley, Belle, 16–26
Born Free, 57
Borneo, 103, 104, 105, 106, 107
Brindamour, Biruté Galdikas. *See*
    Galdikas, Biruté
Brindamour, Rod, 104, 105, 106, 108,
    109, 110, 111, 112
Bronx Zoo (New York), 22, 29, 36
Brookfield Zoo (Chicago), 37
Bryceson, Derek, 49
Buyukmihci, Cavit, 63, 64
Buyukmihci, Hope, 61–71

California, University of, 104
Cambridge University, 102
Cape Haze Marine Laboratory (Flo-
    rida), 87–88, 89, 91
Carrighar, Sally, 14
Cartilaginous fishes, 88
Cempaka (orangutan), 108
Cetaceans, 75, 76
    See also Narwhals; Porpoises;
        Whales
Chimpanzees, 23, 25, 39–50, 53, 96,
    111
    aggression by, 49

Chimpanzees (*continued*)
 and "banana club," 47
 cannibalism of, 49
 as carnivores, 44
 communities of, 42, 46–49
 size of, 42
 as toolmakers, 39–40, 44
 young of, 44–46, 48
China, 28, 29, 30, 36, 37, 104
Chopper (beaver), 61, 62, 63, 64
Clark, Eugenie, 82–92
Coco (gorilla), 97, 99
Conditioning, 77
 defined, 72
 operant, 77–78
Congo, Belgian, 22, 95
Cornell University, 66, 75

David Greybeard (chimpanzee), 40,
 43, 44, 49–50
David Starr Jordan (ship), 81
Diana (panda), 37
Dolphins. *See* Porpoises
Dragons, Komodo, 29

Earthwatch, 133
Eels, garden, 86, 91
Ethology, 13, 14, 81
 as a career. *See* Animal watching
Explorers Club, 36

Fabin (chimpanzee), 47, 48
Fat (beluga), 114
Field Guide to Natural History, 66
Field Museum (Chicago), 29
Fifi (chimpanzee), 44, 123
Figan (chimpanzee), 44, 45, 47, 48
Fish and Wildlife Service, U.S., 85
Flipper (porpoise), 75, 78
Flo (chimpanzee), 44, 47, 48, 123
Fossey, Dian, 93–102, 104

Galapagos tortoise, 22

Galdikas, Biruté, 103–112
Garden eels, 86, 91
Giant panda (*bei-shung*), 28–29, 31,
 32, 33–38
Gibbons, 42
Goliath (chimpanzee), 43, 47
Gombe Stream Research Station, 40,
 43, 46, 47, 48, 49, 50, 95
Goodall, Jane, 23, 39–50, 53, 94, 95,
 96, 104, 123
Goodall, Vanne, 42
Gorillas, 12, 13, 22–25, 42, 93–102,
 111
 cannibalism of, 101
 chest-beating by, 98, 100, 102
 food of, 94, 97, 98
 noseprints of, 98
 as peaceful animals, 94, 100
 size of, 95
 and transfer process, 101
Gouge (beluga), 121
Grannie (owl), 60
Greenbrier (beaver), 70
Guadalupe fur seals, 25
Gulf of St. Lawrence, 114

Habituation, 44, 96, 111
Harkness, Ruth, 27–38
Harkness, William, 29, 36
Hawaii, University of, 75
Hazel (shark), 88
Hebrew University (Israel), 83
Hermaphroditic fish (*Serranus*), 91–
 92
Himalaya Mountains, 27, 28
Holy Nellie (owl), 60
Hornaday, William, 13
Hunter College, 85
Hunting, Hope Buyukmihci's fight
 against, 71

Icarus (gorilla), 100
Ichthyology, 83, 85, 86

Imprinting, 52
Indonesia, 104, 105, 106, 112
Indonesian Forestry Service, 106
Israel, 83

Japan, 87, 91
Johnson, Martin, 22
Johnson, Osa, 22
Jonah, Project, 114, 115, 133
Jungle Book (Kipling), 13

Kai (porpoise), 80–81
Kalimantan, 104, 106
Karen (beluga), 114
Keiki (porpoise), 80
Kenya, 41
Kikos (*Stenella attenuata*), 78
    See also Porpoises
Kipling, Rudyard, 13
Koala bears, 26
Komodo dragons, 29

Laboratories, animals studied in, 13
Lawick, Hugo van, 46, 49
Leakey Foundation, L. S. B., 49, 133
Leakey, Louis, 40, 41, 42, 46, 94, 95,
    100, 104
Leopard, snow, 28
Lorenz, Konrad, 13, 52, 81

Malaysia, 105, 106
Malcolm, Heather, 113–123
Malia (porpoise), 72, 73, 74
Marine Laboratory (Israel), 83
Mbongo (gorilla), 23, 24
McKeever, Kay, 51–60, 123
McKeever, Larry, 53, 59
Mexico, 89, 91
Mickey (tapir), 19–20
Micronesia, 86
Mike (chimpanzee), 47
*Mind and Manners of Wild Animals,
    The* (Hornaday), 13

Morag (wolfhound), 51
Moses sole (*Pardachirus*), 83, 84, 86
Mowatt, Farley, 115

Nairobi (Kenya), natural history
    museum in, 41
Narwhals, 120
National Geographic Society, 99
New York Aquarium, 118
New York Zoological Society, 118
Ngagi (gorilla), 23, 24
Nick (orangutan), 110–111

Ocean Science Theater, at Sea Life
    Park (Hawaii), 72
October (beaver), 63
Olduvai Gorge, 41
Ole Ivory (beluga), 114, 122
Operant conditioning, 77–78
Orangutans (*Pongo pygmaeus*), 25,
    42, 103–112
    food of, 108
    hands of, 109
    intelligence of, 111
    longevity of, 112
    size of, 104
    tools used by, 111, 112
Otter, sea, 40
Outward Bound, Inc., 127, 133
Owl Research and Rehabilitation
    Center, 52
Owls, 12, 51–60
    calcium needed by, 54–55
    as crepuscular birds, 53–54
    hearing of, 54
    nests for, 59–60
    pellets of, 54
    as rat traps, nature's, 57

Pan satyrus (long-haired or eastern
    chimpanzee), 42
Panda, giant (*bei-shung*), 28–29, 31,
    32, 33–38

Pardachirus (Moses sole), 83, 84, 86
Pavlov, Ivan, 77
Peanuts (gorilla), 102
Philippine Islands, 85
Pippard, Leone, 113–123
Plankton, 117
Plectognaths, 86
Pongo pygmaeus. See Orangutans
Porpoise Rescue Foundation, 81
Porpoises (dolphins), 12, 13, 72–81
   brains of, 76
   sounds emitted by, 75
   swimming speed of, 80
   training of, 76–81
President McKinley, U.S.S., 36
Project Jonah, 114, 115, 133
Pryor, Karen, 72–81
Pryor, Tap, 74
Puckerpuss (gorilla), 97, 99

Queens County Aquarium Society, 85

"Rat runners," 13
Rattlesnake, 18
Red apes. *See* Orangutans
Red Sea, 83, 86, 91
Remoras, 90
Rio (orangutan), 108
Robin (beluga), 114, 121
Roosevelt, Kermit, 29, 30, 36
Roosevelt, Theodore (son of President
   Teddy Roosevelt), 29, 30, 36
Rosy (shark), 88

Saguenay River, 115, 119
St. Lawrence River, 115, 120, 121,
   123
San Diego Zoo, 18, 19, 20, 22, 23, 25,
   26
Schaller, George, 94
Scheffer, Victor, 76
Scripps Institute of Oceanography
   (California), 86

Sea canaries. *See* White whales
Sea Life Park (Hawaii), 72, 74, 75,
   77, 80, 81
Sea otter, 40
Seals, 13, 20
   Guadalupe fur, 25
Serranus, 91–92
Shanghai (China), 28, 29, 30, 34, 36
Shaping, in training procedure, 78–79
Shark repellent, 83, 84, 85
Sharks, 74, 82–84, 88–91
   learning by, 89, 90–91
   man-eating, 90
   number of species of, 88
   "sleeping," 89, 90
   in underwater caves, 90, 91
Silverback, as gorilla leader, 98, 100,
   101
Skinner, B. F., 78
Smithsonian Institution, 28
Snow leopard, 28
Sobiarso (orangutan), 108
Sonar system, defined, 75
Spinners, 78
   See also Porpoises
Stanford Primate Facility, 95
Stanford University, 49
Stenella attenuata (kikos), 78
   See also Porpoises
Stimulus control, in training animals,
   79
Student Conservation Corps, 127, 133
Su Lin (panda), 34, 35, 36, 37
Su Sen (panda), 37
Sugito (orangutan), 106–107, 108,
   111
Sumatra, 106
Szechuan Province (China), 28

Tanganyika, Lake, 40, 49
Tanjung Puting Reserve, 105, 112
Tanzania, 40, 41, 49

Tapir, 19–20
Teddy (baboon), 16, 17, 18
Throatpouch (orangutan), 109
Tibet, 28, 29, 31, 37, 38
Tiglet (owl), 51–52, 60, 123
Tortoise, Galapagos, 22
Tsang (hunter on Harkness expedi-
    tion), 32

Uganda, 95, 96
Uncle Bert (gorilla), 100
Unexpected Wildlife Refuge, 62, 65

Virunga Mountains, 94, 95, 101
Virunga National Park, 96
Visoke, Mount, 96

Whale for the Killing, A (Mowatt),
    115
Whales
    baleen, 120
    blue, 118
    fin, 117, 118

humpback, 80
killer, 120
minke, 118
sei, 118
white. *See* White whales
    See also Cetaceans; Narwhals
Wheeper (owl), 52, 57, 60, 123
Whinny (gorilla), 98
Whiskers (beaver), 67
White whales, 113–123
    food of, 122
    hearing of, 114
    at savassats, 120
    size of, 120
    slaughter of, 120
    sounds emitted by, 113–114
William (beluga), 114, 121

Yangtze River, 28
Young, Quentin, 30, 31, 32, 33, 34

Zaire, 94, 95
Zoology, early days of, 12